"White male ideologies have colonized C[...] colonizer-subjugator-enslaver-dominator white male god oppresses women, marginalized peoples, people of color, First Nations peoples, and others. Grace Ji-Sun Kim offers a profound road map for a post-white-male-god church and world. This book is essential reading for a more whole and just future."

Graham Joseph Hill, coauthor with Grace Ji-Sun Kim of *Healing Our Broken Humanity*

"In *When God Became White*, Grace Ji-Sun Kim allows readers to see how religious values and perspectives become skewed when dominated by only one or a few voices, races, or traditions. A not-so-subtle reminder that 'history is written by the victors,' these chapters invite readers to consider the evolution of Christianity from a Jewish movement toward the religion of an empire, and the many ways it was used to promote the superiority of whiteness. This book is a useful resource for both education and introspection around issues that, if left unresolved, will continue to inhibit our best efforts to be people of faith in a multicultural world."

Jay W. Marshall, dean emeritus of the Earlham School of Religion

"This passionate book debunks the collusion of Christianity with whiteness and envisions an inclusive church and community. Grace Ji-Sun Kim uses her personal history to illustrate the devastating results of racism, colonialism, sexism, and classism. It is a valuable resource in our global racial reckoning and for us to imagine beyond a white God."

Kwok Pui-lan, Dean's Professor of Systematic Theology at Candler School of Theology, Emory University

"*When God Became White* is an incredibly comprehensive yet personal and intimate look at the history of whiteness in the church and an excellent example of the power that shows up when silenced voices are heard and held with care. This book is an absolute must-read for all who call themselves Christians today, as the story of Christianity is inexplicably tied up with colonialism, racism, whiteness, and oppression. Grace Ji-Sun Kim is a wise teacher and thoughtful theologian, helping us understand the unjust world that we've created and the steps we can take to heal together. Buy this book and let it guide you toward a better world in which we know and embody the truth that God is love."

Kaitlin B. Curtice, author of *Native* and *Living Resistance*

"A timely book that reflects the shifting of Christianity from the West to the Global South. Grace Ji-Sun Kim's excellent book dismantles white imperial theology and supremacy that provide legitimacy for settler colonialism, racism, and patriarchy. The book tackles the biggest challenge facing the church today while providing a fresh and liberating vision for a nonwhite and nongendered God, an inclusive Christian community, and a world based on justice."

Mitri Raheb, president of Dar al-Kalima University in Bethlehem, Palestine

"I have long been nourished and energized by Grace Ji-Sun Kim's body of work, and this book is no exception. A powerful and liberating exposé, *When God Became White* is the book I wish had existed when I was growing up as a young Black woman in a white-Christian world. Even more, I wish the Christians who purported to shepherd me had read this book. I'll be recommending *When God Became White* to every Christian leader who has ears to hear."

Christena Cleveland, director of the Center for Justice + Renewal and author of *God Is a Black Woman*

"Grace Ji-Sun Kim's *When God Became White* is a must-read for all Christians. Those committed to being antiracists themselves and rooting racism out of the church have much to learn from the history and theology of *When God Became White*. Grace Ji-Sun Kim weaves her personal experience together with Christian theology and practice to demonstrate how God became white and male, why making God into a white man is idolatrous, and what Christians can do to reclaim God from racists, misogynists, and Christian nationalists in order to truly honor and worship the God of justice, peace, and love."

Liz Theoharis, director of the Kairos Center for Religions, Rights, and Social Justice at Union Theological Seminary and co-chair of the Poor People's Campaign: A National Call for Moral Revival

"Grace Ji-Sun Kim's *When God Became White* is a critical gift to the Western church. Through historical record, personal testimony and postcolonial vision, Kim guides readers into the profound and necessary work of dethroning a white male God. Drawing from Korean conceptions of God, she then seeds new vision for the God of all, even as she helps us see more clearly the image of God that is in all."

Lisa Sharon Harper, president and founder of Freedom Road, author of *Fortune: How Race Broke My Family and the World—and How to Repair It All*

"Grace Ji-Sun Kim invites us on a journey to *teshuvah/metanoia*—changing our theological minds and returning to the good news of a God who loved us enough to enter human history as a Brown outsider on a mission to dismantle empire. Grace tackles the ways racism has deformed the church by problematizing white theology, sharing how these theologies wounded her immigrant family, and offering a map to find our way home to the God we know exists. Grace urges us to break the chains that bind the church to a gendered white God by engaging in theological wrestling that will likely bless us and transform the church."

Jacqui Lewis, senior minister and public theologian, Middle Church, and author of *Fierce Love*

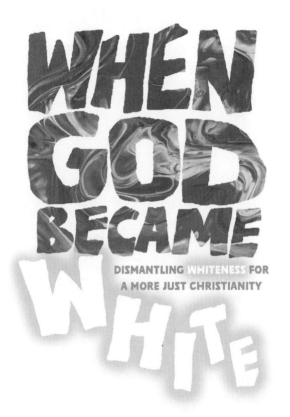

WHEN GOD BECAME WHITE

DISMANTLING WHITENESS FOR
A MORE JUST CHRISTIANITY

GRACE JI-SUN KIM

FOREWORD BY DAVID P. GUSHEE

ivp

An imprint of InterVarsity Press
Downers Grove, Illinois

InterVarsity Press
P.O. Box 1400 | Downers Grove, IL 60515-1426
ivpress.com | email@ivpress.com

Scripture quotations, unless otherwise noted, are from the New Revised Standard Version, Updated Edition.
Copyright © 2021 National Council of Churches of Christ in the United States of America. Used by permission.
All rights reserved worldwide.

While any stories in this book are true, some names and identifying information may have been changed to
protect the privacy of individuals.

The publisher cannot verify the accuracy or functionality of website URLs used in this book beyond the date
of publication.

Cover design: Cindy Kiple
Images: © DevidDO / iStock / Getty Images Plus

ISBN 978-1-5140-0939-0 (print) | ISBN 978-1-5140-0940-6 (digital)

Printed in the United States of America ∞

Library of Congress Cataloging-in-Publication Data
A catalog record for this book is available from the Library of Congress.

31   30   29   28   27   26   25   24 | 12   11   10   9   8   7   6   5   4   3   2   1

For Theodore, Elisabeth, and Joshua,

and to their future filled with hope and love.

May they know a better and

a more just world apart from whiteness.

CONTENTS

Foreword

DAVID P. GUSHEE

In the book you are about to read, Grace Ji-Sun Kim does three very important things. First, she offers a sustained critique not just of whiteness but of white maleness as an ideology and a theology. Second, she tells parts of her own story as a Korean immigrant first to Canada and then the United States. Third, she offers a way of thinking about God that can contribute to the dismantling of inherited theology that she seeks.

I want to say a word about each of these elements.

Critique of the white male God. The reader would do well to understand the multiple dimensions of the critique. Dr. Kim is arguing that, at least after the conversion of Constantine and the Romanization, then Europeanization, of an originally Middle Eastern Jewish movement called Christianity, that religion came under the dominance of European men of power both political and religious. Eventually, in the colonial era, these men carried their particular version of Christianity all over the world. Gradually, they came to define themselves as racially white over against other "lesser" races of people that they were encountering, conquering, enslaving, and killing. They also came to define their God as someone remarkably like themselves—the greatest of all white male conquerors.

The whiteness that Professor Kim is critiquing, and the white male God that she is trying to dismantle, is this ideological God who, perhaps in somewhat more subtle ways than in the sixteenth and seventeenth centuries, remains the God not just of today's white male Christians but of many believers of color whose minds and souls have been colonized by the white male God of conqueror-enslaver-dominator-missionary Christianity. This is a God who supports both continued oppression of people of color but also their own self-abnegation.

A Korean immigrant's painful journey. In what I experienced as the most deeply affecting parts of the book, Dr. Kim describes significant parts of her own difficult journey. This is the story of a young girl brought with her family from Korea to Canada and plunged with her family into a life of poverty and culture shock. The initial involvement and then conversion of her family to a rigidly conservative, white-missionary-influenced version of Christianity is also powerfully recounted here. These stories put flesh on the bones of Professor Kim's account of the white male God. For it was this God whom her family was led to worship and serve. It was this God who underwrote the severe patriarchy of her family system. And it was breaking with this God that has been such a painful but liberating transition in Dr. Kim's own life. One sees the many losses that she has sustained in finally sloughing off the authoritarian white male God with whom she spent her childhood and adolescence and who apparently still rules in her family or origin.

Theologizing a post-white-male God. Professor Kim offers suggestions of how to think theologically in a way that can combat this inherited ideology-theology, so destructive in its consequences both for oppressors and oppressed. The reader will see that her basic moves—developed more fully in others of her works—are to identify strands of the Bible in which God is imagined in ways that are nongendered and nonpatriarchal. She identifies the Shekinah strand of the Hebrew Bible, the Hokhmah/Sophia wisdom strand suggested in both the Hebrew Bible and New Testament, and the overall biblical theme of God as Spirit as three such moves. She emphasizes themes like visibility, dignity for all, inclusion, and community. She suggests that we think of breath, light, wind, and vibration when we think of God. In these suggestions she finds points of connection with Korean words and concepts as well. The God she invites us to imagine is not absent from Scripture but is downplayed in much dominant Christian theology.

This book makes a significant contribution to contemporary Christian theology and has substantial implications for ethics as well. I urge even—especially!—those who may not feel ready for the strength of the critique Dr. Kim offers to ask God to help you lay down any spirit of defensiveness and instead to be open to the breath of inspiration and new life.

Introduction

WHITE CHRISTIANITY

I am going to say something that may sound extreme, but if you stay with me, you'll understand why it's true. Everything is connected to race.

Race might be considered a social construct, but we can see how race affects culture, history, religion, employment, laws, and ideas. Race influences how we act and behave daily. It forms our perceptions of each other and affects how we act in different circumstances. The societal views of immigrants, Natives, and refugees have a profound impact on our ability to relate to people of different races. It has also greatly influenced Christianity and our understanding of God.

When I began to realize the enormous impact of race, I knew it was important for me to study race, racism, and ethnicity to understand how we have come to construct a white Christianity and a white God. This is how I began my explorations for writing this book. My own life has been impacted by race relations because it has ultimately defined me, had a negative influence on me daily, and has formed my own understandings of a white Christianity and a white God.

When I was growing up in the 1970s in London, Ontario, we began elementary school each morning by reciting the Lord's

Prayer and singing the national anthem. It was very clear to me as an immigrant child that Canada was a Christian country and that I needed to become a Christian if I was going to fit into my new home. Our family did not have any religious affiliations when we first immigrated in 1975. But a very nice young Korean couple started asking my older sister and me to go to church with them. My sister and I eventually began attending and had a lot of fun at church. We met other Korean kids our age and we made lots of new friends there.

Soon, my parents started attending church with us as other Korean immigrants encouraged them to join us at the local Korean church. They were happy to meet other Korean immigrant families at the church and it became a community for us. We did not know anyone when we moved to Canada, so the church became our extended family. We held birthday parties, weddings, anniversaries, and any other celebrations at church. It was a place for us to become a family with other Korean immigrant families.

Through attending church, our family eventually became Christians. We ended up attending a Korean Presbyterian church on Sundays, but mid-week and on Friday nights, my parents dropped my sister and me off at a white Baptist church and a Christian and Missionary Alliance church for Bible studies, fellowship, and worship. Church soon overtook our lives; everything was planned around church events.

I made lots of friends at these different churches. Part of the purpose for attending so many different churches was that, in a way, it provided free English classes. My parents were worried that our English wasn't good enough for us to excel at school, and they thought by being immersed in white churches, we would learn to speak better and to understand the white culture we were living in.

I was definitely informed by this experience. The churches all impacted my perception of God, who Jesus was, and what I was supposed to do with my life. When I think about my childhood and how I raised my own three children, I see a world of a difference. One day when I was trying to wake my youngest, who was a teen at the time, I nudged him over and over until he said, "What?!" I told him to hurry up and get ready for church. He complained, "Again?" I said, "What you do you mean again? This is the first time going to church this week."

If my children understood the number of churches I went to during a week, they would be happy they only had to go to church once a week.

I was an Asian immigrant girl who grew up with a white Jesus. And that wasn't just at church. We had a white Jesus hanging on the wall in our living room—the extremely popular *Head of Christ* by artist Warner Sallman. I never found out where my dad got this famous print, but I am certain he didn't buy it. We were too poor to buy even food and basic clothing, never mind nonessentials like decor. I am sure my dad must have found it someplace near the garbage or some stranger at his factory gave it to him for free.

My mother was a strong woman of faith, and she loved the picture of Jesus and admired it with a huge smile. She felt the best place to hang this print of Jesus surrounded by a cheap, fake wood frame was over our couch so you could see him when you entered the apartment. She thought if you sat on the couch, the "blessing" of Jesus would come down on you. Sallman's picture of a white Jesus was prominent in our home, and I believed that is how Jesus really looked.

My mother treated this print image as if it were a holy art piece and carefully packed it every time we moved. That image was one of the first things unpacked in the new place. In every place we lived, she hung it behind the living room couch so we could see the image of Jesus every day and any visitors to the home would see it immediately.

The white Jesus on our wall was a depiction to me of how God looked as well. I pictured God as an old white man, just as everyone else did. There was no reason to question that notion. It was everywhere: in paintings, stained-glass windows, and story-books. I never questioned it. I didn't even think twice about whether Jesus was white or not. It was not in my consciousness to question anything that was taught by my mother or the church. Both pushed a white Jesus, and I just took it as the truth.

I have no idea where my mother's beloved white Jesus picture is now. It is probably in a dump somewhere. My sister threw out many of our belongings every time we moved homes. But the damage is done. It is so difficult to rid ourselves of these deeply embedded images of a white male God that were engrained in us at home, at church, and in society. But, I have now come to see the consequences of believing in a white male God.

What I didn't know then that I know now is how influential that picture was on my own theology and faith development. That image of a white Jesus was imprinted on my brain and body so that I could not even question whether Jesus actually looked like that. It was a given, as it was the most famous picture of Jesus. I went to visit family in Korea twice during my youth, and even my family members there had the same picture of the white Jesus in their homes. The Korean churches also had the same picture of white Jesus. Furthermore, when I traveled to India during my seminary years, all the churches that I visited had this same white Jesus picture. This confirmed to me that this must be the real Jesus, as it is universally understood to be the image of Christ.

I just took it for granted that Sallman's *Head of Christ* must be the real thing. I never questioned it until much later in my adult life. This was also partly due to the reverence that my mom had for the cheap printed copy of the image in our home. She would look at it as if in prayer. To her it was an indication that ours was a Christian home, and this meant the world to her.

My mom was a very conservative evangelical Christian. Though we attended the First London Presbyterian Church, the denomination didn't mean much to her or our entire family. We were more concerned about preserving our conservative Christianity in any way, shape, or form. She loved this image of a white Jesus, and thus everyone else in the family was expected to love this image too. In Korean culture, you don't question parents or elders; you just obey. To question the validity of this painting felt bad, as if I were questioning my mother's beliefs and understandings.

My family's story is the same as many of my Christian friends. Sallman's image may not have been as prominently displayed as it was in our house, but it was in their homes to signify that they were Christians. We all lived with this white representation of Jesus.

Living in white spaces as a nonwhite person is exhausting. It is so depleting that it sucks the life out of you. I have experienced racism throughout my life. I have tried to understand racism and how it functions, and I have learned that the only way to fight it is to address whiteness and dismantle it.

After growing up in an environment that reinforced the whiteness of God, not just with the Sallman's image but also through other biblical and church teachings and practices, it was a devastating revelation that these images of a white Jesus might be wrong and even intentionally created to reinforce white supremacy in Christianity, society, and culture. This book is about the religious journey I took to make sense of my own experiences and place them in context. It explores the emergence of a white Jesus and what the implications of this are on racialized minorities. In this process, I came to understand how whiteness has corrupted our understanding of each other and God. If we are to overcome the devastating effects of whiteness, we need to move forward and adopt a theology of visibility so we can embrace the other and live in peace with our neighbors.

I hope my questions and challenges of a white Christianity will help you in your own explorations of faith, spirituality, and God. Please join me on this inner journey of unpacking whiteness, white Christianity, and a white God.

WHITENESS

For centuries, the classification of race has been a powerful tool for white male lawmakers, leaders, church ministers, and the privileged to maintain their power and the status quo. But how did it start? Why was one group able to claim so much authority and wield so much control over other groups? And what could have been done to stop them?

In exploring whiteness we come to see how Jesus became white and the faith of his followers took on a profoundly racist bent. From the early Christian beginnings under the Roman Empire to the conservative Christian right of today, a white male God has been at the center. This projection of their own identity onto who God is by powerful white men has tainted the instructions found in the Bible that we are to love all people equally.

Those in power believe that they are divinely placed there and have been ordained to lead the church and to define the God we are to follow. They suppose that their understanding of God is the truth, they preach their understanding as truth, and they fail to recognize that they are attributing their own self-serving desires to God.

The whitewashed "good news" spread throughout the world thanks to colonialism, crusades, and missionaries who infected others with whiteness under the guise of Christianity. The propagation of this myth of a white God and a white Jesus has had a devastating effect that has rippled across the globe through generations. Whiteness helps readers understand the origins of this distortion of our shared history and identify the ways in which their own experiences as well as those of minorities have been deeply affected. This book also identifies why this myth of a white God must change and where change starts.

BOOK OUTLINE

This book is composed of nine chapters. Chapter one is "Encountering Whiteness." Race has become a powerful tool for lawmakers, leaders, church ministers, and the privileged to maintain their own power and the status quo. To understand how the world is stratified and structured according to race, we need to unpack the origins of whiteness and its implications for the church, Christianity, and theology. This chapter provides a historical and social overview of how the concept of race emerged and was sustained to firmly hold power for white male European enslavers.

Chapter two is on the problem of whiteness. Whiteness is not factual but has been used as a tool of destruction in communities of color in so many dangerous ways as it leads to white privilege and white supremacy. Whiteness is not a race, and due to its dangerous use, it needs to be eliminated from society if we are to achieve any form of liberation and freedom for all groups of oppressed people of color. White supremacy believes that whites are superior over people of color, and it upholds unjust social structures that exist to benefit white people.

Chapter three, "Becoming a White Christianity," is where I discuss the long history of how Christianity became white and maintained its whiteness. White Christianity spread throughout the world through the "good" work of white missionaries who went to Asia, Africa, South America, and all parts of the world to share what was essentially the "good news" of whiteness. As we study the history of Christianity's whiteness, we need to question and reexamine what its implications are for people of color, immigrants, and refugees who come from all over the world to the United States.

The fourth chapter, "A Missiology of Whiteness," examines how whiteness was part of the white missionary's message when they went to Asia to share the good news of Jesus Christ. The message of whiteness and the good news were so intertwined that at times, the messages became one. Asians accepted this white gospel and never questioned it. The acceptance of a white Christian message is in part due to Orientalism, which views Asia in a stereotyped way that embodies a colonialist attitude. Orientalism emphasizes, exaggerates, and distorts Asians as compared to Europeans. This has big implications for Asians and how the West perceives and treats the East.

The fifth chapter, "Christianity and Whiteness," examines how racism and discrimination go hand in hand with whiteness and Christianity. My own immigration story shows how whiteness has shaped my rejection of my Asian culture and identity and accepted a white Christianity. I was literally pushed to accept a white culture that emphasized the goodness and priority of whiteness in Christianity. This results in white supremacy, white Christian nationalism, and a white Christianity, to the detriment of people of color.

Chapter six focuses on how we got a white Jesus. When we question the identity of Jesus, we see that over time Jesus *became* white, and this has great implications for church and society. As

Christians continue to worship a white Jesus, we must discern how we can correct this error as it affects all aspects of society, whether one is religious, Christian, or not.

Chapter seven highlights the dangers of worshiping a white God. White Christian power reinforces a white masculine almighty God. The patriarchal notion of God creates a context where racism is a bold part of the everyday life of the church. As the center of Christianity, God being white implies that whites are the center of humanity and that God's concerns and God's desires center on white people at the expense of people of color. This has damaging consequences for people of color who experience grave injustices due to racism, discrimination, and xenophobia.

Chapter eight, "The Problem of a White Gendered God," looks at how a male God has subjugated women. In addition to the whiteness of God is the gendering of God as a man. In light of sexism, sexual violence, and atrocities committed against women in society and in Christianity, it is necessary to move away from this gendered white understanding of God. A gendered white male God legitimizes and promotes patriarchy, and subordinates and problematizes women in church and society. A nongendered God loves all, welcomes all, and empowers disempowered women.

Chapter nine works toward liberating whiteness. Through the invention of a white Jesus and a white male God, the reality of a white Christian empire is steeped in many different problems, which have spread throughout the world. Today, Christians need to engage in racial justice work to reverse the damages of creating a white Christianity and a white Jesus. We need to challenge the white male Christian empire and work toward an all-embracing kin-dom. A liberative way of understanding God is to view God as Spirit. Spirit is genderless and nonwhite, which helps all of us to learn to embrace one another. We need to heed the Spirit's urgent call to engage in this justice work before more people are murdered, disenfranchised, oppressed, and pushed to the underside of society.

The last chapter, "Embracing a Nonwhite and Nongendered God," deals with the applications of how to move forward in dismantling whiteness and a white male God. It offers tools and actions that we can all take to make a difference in our lives, church, and society. Through rewriting liturgy, discipleship, and justice work, we can work toward a better world where all are equal, and all are accepted as created in the image of God. This is a source of much hope as we seek a day when we can embrace God and embrace one another.

Note: when we explore the history of colonialism and whiteness, we necessarily must address the realities of atrocities that have been perpetrated against vulnerable peoples. Some material, especially in chapter three, includes accounts of sexual assault, violence, and trauma. My hope is that reckoning with the legacy of the past will aid us in confronting present realities.

1

ENCOUNTERING WHITENESS

We have been using the classification of race to benefit those with power in this country since its inception. It has become an essential tool for lawmakers, leaders, church ministers, and others in the privileged class to maintain the status quo. The only way we will understand just how effective racial categorization is for those who hold power is to look at its origin—the history of racialization and the troubles it has caused people of color. The concept of race emerged and was sustained for European plantation owners to justify the existing power dynamic, and through this lens we can begin to understand the problem of whiteness.

IMMIGRATING TO WHITENESS

It was my dad's idea to leave Korea in 1975 and take his young family with him. Korea had suffered the devastating destruction from the Korean War, yielding a climate that was economically and politically difficult and frighteningly unstable. The Korean economy was struggling, and my dad felt it was in the best interest of his two young girls, ages six and five, for him to take his family and immigrate to America. In the 1970s it was easier to gain access to Canada than to the United States, as fewer Koreans wanted to live in Canada. Thus, my dad chose this easier route with the intention of moving to the States soon thereafter.

We immigrated in January 1975. We landed in Toronto, and within weeks, we moved to London, Ontario, a small city two hours west of Toronto. We moved to a run-down apartment, which was bug infested and dirty. I remember January being icy cold. London is located in a snow belt area, and so much snow fell in 1975 that there was snow up to my waist. Often, as I walked to school, I would lose my shoes in the deep snow and have to retrace my steps to retrieve them. I hated the cold, and my small, frail body could not take the harsh winter winds and freezing cold temperatures. We didn't have any family or relatives besides the four of us, which left me feeling terribly alienated and alone.

Starting kindergarten in the middle of the year caused anguish, dread, and deep pain. What should have been the best school experience with days full of games, singing, making new friends, and no homework was neither easy nor enjoyable for me.

I went through two profound challenges in the first two weeks of kindergarten. The first was a deep culture shock, which shook me to the core of my being. Everything was new to me; I couldn't adjust to the cold, the language, the city, and our new apartment. As a society, we believe that children are able to adjust quickly to new situations, cultures, and contexts, but that was not the case for me. I didn't know any English and felt deeply ashamed, miserable, and frustrated for not being able to understand or speak this new language during my first few months of school. Before we immigrated, my sister and I pretended to speak English and played wild make-believe games with each other. We had no idea it would be so difficult to learn the language and adapt to the new environment.

My second challenge was encounters with racism. I looked very different from all the white kids in my class, and my looks and my Koreanness were an easy target for their ridicule. It didn't matter whether I understood English or not; I felt their hatred and ridicule without comprehending a word they said. Kids would place their fingers on their eyes and pull them out or sideways and laugh and make fun of my small Asian eyes. They would also mimic Chinese intonations and phonology and yell out "ching chong" or "ching chang chong." These hateful ethnic slurs and pejorative terms were used to mock me and make me feel small and unworthy. The taunts and eye pulls were not a one-time event either; they occurred almost daily during recess and lunch break. Teachers saw what the other kids were doing to me, but they ignored it. It was racism, and it seemed to be sanctioned by the adults.

I wanted to get rid of my Koreanness, but I couldn't. I could not remove the yellow skin I was born in. I could not change my smaller and thinner eyelids to look like the white girls in class. I knew that I could not single-handedly stop the racism that I was experiencing daily.

My dad used to tell me all throughout my childhood and even into my adulthood how lucky we were to have immigrated to North America. But I couldn't see how it was better. Our family lived in a run-down apartment building ironically named Frontenac Apartments. In Montreal, one of the most upscale hotels is called Château Frontenac, but our two-bedroom apartment was nothing like the elite, beautiful, and romantic hotel. It was a dirty, run-down building known for being a place where immigrants lived for a short while until they found somewhere better. There were probably around ten Korean immigrant families living in these Frontenac apartments during the seventies and eighties. One by one, they all moved away, and we were one of the last families to leave because my parents didn't have the money to find to a better place.

I was afraid the cockroaches would crawl up my legs while I slept. I was afraid of stepping on them in the dark if I went to the bathroom during the night. I was afraid they roamed over our plates, bowls, and cutlery. I was afraid I'd never get away from them, and that was a difficult thing to get over as I grew up.

We had no new furniture except for the twin beds my mom bought for my sister and me. Everything else was hand-me-down furniture or came from Goodwill or the dumpster. My dad would bring trashy furniture into our apartment to salvage, so when my mom bought the two cheap beds, there was a firestorm in our household and my parents fought for days about her spending the money. Ultimately, my sister and I were allowed to keep our beds, which was a treat as we had been sleeping on the floor on top of blankets for years.

Nothing in this place that was supposed to be the land of opportunity was easy, and some things were really painful. I told my dad that I wished I had grown up in my homeland. I wished I didn't have to explain myself to everyone: that I was born in Korea, ate different foods, and spoke a different language in our home. I didn't want to keep explaining why I looked different and why I had a *Konglish* (Korean/English) accent. I could not understand why he felt we were better off with this kind of life than what we would have had back home.

RACE

Words are vital. Words convey our thoughts and ideas to the outside world. Words also form our thoughts and concepts *about* the world and ourselves. Those who hold power have the capability to change minds, ideas, and processes of thinking through words. This is the power of words.

The study of race reveals how those who hold power have such enormous ability to change worldviews, affect laws, change behaviors, and even change our understanding of God. This is the impact of words, and powerful people must be mindful of their power as we discuss race and race making (how race is created), and the consequences of both. The notion of race is based not on biology but on social meanings that are created and re-created due to changing contexts. The concept of race was created mainly by Europeans in the sixteenth century and is based on socially constructed beliefs about the inherent superiority and inferiority of groups of people. Studies on race critique the notion as lacking any scientific clarity and specificity, as it is informed by historical, social, cultural, and political values and not any biological terms.[1] However, white people have tried to argue that race is based on biology as some have tried to measure brain size and prove that their brains are larger and hence they are superior to others.

No person of any race or ethnicity has a biological or spiritual claim to being better than anyone else. Race has served to separate society into different levels for the benefit of a few people who have been defined as white, to the misfortune of anyone considered nonwhite or of color. "Although race is something imagined (or constructed), its effects are real. From lifespans to salary to where you live, race has a measurable impact on a person's quality of life."[2] We need to recognize the problem of this concept of race and bring it into our mainstream conversation and thought.

We have socially constructed the category of race based on perceptions of different skin color. We have created an inequitable social and economic relationship that is structured and reproduced through skin color, class, gender, and nation.[3] Race was created by and for white people and in service of white supremacists. As a social construct, it has huge ramifications on American society, economics, politics, and religion. Race is not a benign category; it is an oppressive structure and understanding. For people in positions of power, *race* became an important term as it played a role in the construction of law or rules for social interaction between white people and people of color.

ENSLAVEMENT HISTORY AND RACIAL IDENTITY

American race relations emerged from the intersection of three significant events in history: the conquest of Native Americans, the forced importation of Africans, and the coming together of Europeans, Asians, and Latinos.[4] The intersection of these significant events led to the need to divide and distinguish people according to race. This was carefully accomplished by those in power to serve themselves and maintain their power.

We can get a clearer understanding of how racism, white supremacy, and discrimination are maintained in our society by looking into the changing dynamics of racial identity. Racism is part of the daily lives of people of color, and I experience it all too often. We can see how racism is used to subordinate people of color as we begin to comprehend how white identity emerged in our society.

Before the seventeenth century, Europeans did not think of themselves as belonging to a white race. Instead, they viewed themselves as belonging to different parts or regions in Europe and had a very different perception of race and racialization. But once this concept of white race was shown to be advantageous to Europeans and enslavers, it began to reshape and redefine their world. The impact of this is still felt today. Europeans have only recently started to think of themselves as belonging to a white race,[5] and it has only come as they realized they could profit financially, socially, politically, and religiously. White race and white identity have not been constant but have changed over time to accommodate the variances of social change and context.

Race and *ethnicity* are sometimes used interchangeably by the general public, but we must note that they are two different terms. *Race* is a categorization of people into groups based on shared physical or social characteristics. Races are often viewed as distinct and different within a society. The term *race* became more common during the sixteenth century when it was used to refer to groups of various kinds. *Ethnicity*, on the other hand, encompasses a larger group of categories, such as heritage, language, nationality, culture, customs, and religion. Both terms are used to describe and categorize people.

White identity was solidified in the seventeenth century by justifying African enslavement. Robert Baird notes,

> The invention of a white racial identity was motivated by plantation owners in the West Indies and in the American colonies who depended on European indentured servants for labor who were forced to work for long periods in the plantations but were made 'free' when they paid off their debt to the plantation owners. These servants were considered chattel and were often treated brutally. But, since many of them became Christian, they could not be held in lifetime captivity unless they were criminals or prisoners of war.[6]

The expiration date on indentured servitude and not a lifetime captivity created problems for the plantation owners who needed a constant supply of laborers so that they could continue to make huge profits and live their comfortable and lavish lifestyle. They needed more laborers, and the transatlantic enslavement of Africans proved to be a good alternative to European indentured servants.

An increase in worldwide demand for tobacco, cotton, and sugar led seventeenth-century colonials to seek a large labor force to meet market demands from Europe and America. Native Americans proved difficult to subjugate, and European Christians were becoming more and more reluctant to enslave other Christians.[7] Around 1640, the working and living conditions of indentured servants began to affect the numbers of those willing to enter the arrangement. The loss of this source of labor drove landowners to seek new forms of labor that would be cost efficient and profitable. With the loss of European indentured workers and the need for a high volume of cheap labor, the colonialists turned to Africans, which became advantageous and profitable.

Colonial Europeans found that Africans were knowledgeable about tropical agriculture, skilled in iron working, and immune to Old World diseases. They believed them to be docile and already conditioned to subjugation by African tribal chiefs. During a 110-year period (1700–1810), approximately six million Africans were transported to the New World. In order to legitimize the status differences, laws were enacted to enslave them for life. White European indentured servants were afforded an end to their servitude; however, it wasn't until 1863 when the Emancipation Proclamation was signed into law[8] that Africans and their descendants were released from captivity. Enslaved Africans were without freedom in America for more than 244 years.

The enslaved people lived under harsh environments and strict laws. Due to some uprisings, plantation owners were afraid that a violent rebellion might occur. In order to preempt that, each colony passed a series of laws governing the behaviors of enslaved Africans, which were known as slave codes.[9] They were strict laws that covered movements, marriage, gatherings, trade, punishment, and education. Essentially, every aspect of their daily lives was restricted. Enslavement was violent, cruel, degrading, and inhumane. Violence was committed against people's bodies and minds to keep them in line with fear. This was a daily war carried out against Africans to ensure they lacked power and freedom, and to maintain the economic, political, cultural, and religious power held by the European colonists.[10]

Christian religious identity was at first very important for the development of the English slave trade as it was a way to make one group "evil" and another group "good." Africans were perceived as infidels and enemies of Christian nations, which helped justify their enslavement and the violence committed against them. But by the 1670s, Christian missionaries, including Quaker George Fox, insisted that enslaved Africans convert to Christianity. This posed a problem for the plantation owners. If enslaved Africans became Christians, they were no longer enemies of Christendom, and it would be difficult to enslave them. Some tried to block enslaved Africans from converting to Christianity, but when this didn't work, they passed laws disqualifying baptism as grounds for freedom. Since baptism seals the Christian with the spiritual mark of belonging to Christ and makes everyone equal in the sight of God, slave owners were afraid they would lose the upper hand. This presented the need for another category to prevent the enslaved Africans from becoming free. It was a pivotal moment, and a new category of identity was created: white people.

THE CREATION OF WHITE PEOPLE

Toward the end of the seventeenth century, using Christianity as a means of separating the enslaver and the enslaved was no longer useful with Africans being evangelized. The term *white people* emerged to differentiate these groups and to maintain and sustain African enslavement. Laws that regulated enslaved and servant behavior, such as the 1681 Servant Act in Jamaica, described the privileged class as whites rather than Christians. The establishment of white identity as a legal category created a powerful distinction between indentured Europeans and enslaved Africans. Colonists began to think of themselves as white[11] and to believe that their whiteness elevated them in such a way that they could justify the enslavement of Africans.

The creation of white people worked, and plantation owners continued to profit and live lavishly. It was a stroke of genius for those of European descent, and we feel this bifurcation of identity even today, as race is still used as a defining characteristic for value and power.

Before the late 1600s, Europeans did not use the term *Black* to reference any group of people. However, with the racialization of enslavement around 1680, many looked for a term to differentiate between the enslaved and the enslavers. Thus the terms *white* and *Black* were used to represent and differentiate racial categories.[12] European landowners came to understand that whiteness was a powerful weapon that allowed them to continue transatlantic capitalism for securing labor. While plantation owners extended privilege to the white poor to differentiate them from enslaved Africans, the idea of being white wasn't concrete— it was fluid and it meant different things in different parts of America and around the world.[13] Over time, this meant changes as to who was white and who was not, but through it all it was clear that white people had power over others.

VARIATIONS IN WHITE PEOPLE

Before the mid-nineteenth century, American society accepted that there was more than one white race. Many Americans were viewed as white, but they were not all the same type of white people as there were inferior and superior whites. The Saxons were viewed as superior while the Celts were understood to be inferior. As such, Saxons were regarded highly as they were viewed as smart, lively, clearheaded, Protestant, and attractive. On the other hand, Celts were viewed as unintelligent, reckless, intoxicated, Catholic, and unattractive. This dichotomy was useful to those in the superior white group as it helped to elevate themselves and present themselves as better. Hence when the Irish participated in the mass immigration due to the 1840s famine, many nativists spread an anti-Catholic bigotry right to the end of the century. This helped reinforce the superior whites and suppressed the inferior whites. This history shows that at first, the Irish were not even considered white and were sometimes referred to as "negroes turned inside out."[14] But perceptions have changed and today the Irish are viewed as white people and superior over Blacks and other people of color. This example of the change of perception of the Irish shows that there is fluidity in the concept of whiteness.

Other events in history produced new forms of racial classification and identity. When waves of poor Eastern and Southern European immigrants arrived, new racial classifications were birthed. What followed was the "northern Italian" race and the "southern Italian" race to help differentiate between the superior north from the inferior south. Even though they were all technically white, the Irish, Italians, Jews, and Greeks were classified as inferior and, at times, not even classified as whites. It was not until the 1970s that these groups were considered white. With the rise in interracial marriages, the idea of fluidity in racial identity was employed more and more to reveal the fluidity of racial categorizations and identities. As a result, by the early twentieth century, the descendants of Irish immigrants decided to elevate inferior Celts into superior northern Europeans. This helped them to be separate from Blacks and other people of color. However, World War I lowered Americans' affection for the Saxons due to their association with Germans and Nazism but then increased the popularity and likability of a new term— *Nordic*—which was free from any Germanic associations. Therefore, white identity changed throughout history according to the context, different situations, and world affairs.

By the 1940s, anthropologists decided to simplify all these different categorizations of people and announced that there are only three classifications: Caucasoid (White), Mongoloid (Asian), and Negroid (Black).[15] With these three classifications, everyone of European descent was now considered white, and there were no longer any distinctions for Saxons, Celts, Southern Italians, or Eastern European Jews. They all just became one large group and were viewed as white. In addition, there were no longer any divisions of superior or inferior whites, and all whites became superior to people of color. Since the 1940s, there have only been very minor modifications to these classifications.

In this racial identity, whites do not carry the burden of race in America as white people perceive whiteness as a neutral racial identity.[16] White people are viewed as the norm, and everyone else is one or more steps away from the normative in society. This neutral racial stance is beneficial and powerful as it pits other racialized groups as inferior and deficient. The view of whiteness as neutral only reinforced white people's superior status over everyone else.

WHITENESS

Racial identity is fluid and changes over time because *white* is a relational term, and it is present only in opposition to other classifications in the racial pyramid, which is ordered and created by whiteness. By defining "others" as inferior, subordinate, and less than, whiteness is able to define itself. Whiteness is a socially and politically constructed idea that is distinct but not separate from ideas of class, country, gender, and sexuality.

White is a created category of race that has no biological/scientific foundation. *Whiteness*, on the other hand, is a compelling and convincing powerful social construct with tangible, destructive, and violent effects. Whiteness is a cultural space with political power and privilege with a goal and an agenda to keep people of color marginalized, oppressed, and subordinated. Whiteness is a learned behavior that is multidimensional, complex, extensive, and systemic, which becomes a powerful tool for white people.[17] Whiteness is not just skin color but goes beyond it as an idea based on beliefs, values, and attitudes with an unequal distribution of power, influence, and privilege based on skin color. It is about how the powerful determine who has the privilege of being white and who does not and hence push them down the ladder of hierarchy. Whiteness becomes a construct created by those in power to maintain their own power, dominance, and the status quo. It keeps whites at the top of the hierarchy, possessing power, supremacy, status, privilege, wealth, and domination.

Whiteness groups all people in the United States of different ethnicities (Irish, English, French, German, Italian, and so forth) with fair skin as one people. The purpose is not to find a common ethnic name for these people, but rather, whiteness is a term of "ethnic erasure." Consequently, the distinct histories and ethnicities of people in this group are erased by being made "white." This term *white* creates privileged groups in relation to all "nonwhite" people on the basis of whiteness.[18] Whiteness patterns social interaction and social organization between whites and people of color. It builds barriers between groups of people as either privileged or marginalized and unfavorable.

Since whiteness is constructed and maintained by powerful leaders to maintain their own place in society, Lisa Sharon Harper calls whiteness a "phantom." Whiteness is elusive because white people do not have a common struggle, similar story, or common people[19] as their identities get melted together. No one can challenge whiteness for fear of retaliation for opposing whiteness. Whiteness holds its power tightly and maintains its power with fierceness, which in turn continues to hurt communities of color.

The construct of color is a means of maintaining power by whites. Africans do not think of themselves as Black, but when Africans come to the United States, they begin to be labeled and identified as Black. Similarly, we Asians do not think of ourselves as yellow when we are born. We do not see our skin color as yellow until we leave Asia and white people begin to label us as yellow. White people disliked Asians and created the racial metaphor "yellow peril" to keep us subordinate and subservient. Yellow peril suggests Asians are an existential danger to the West. There is no proof of any danger, but the fear arises from a baseless misconception and erroneous belief of Asians as yellow people, which is just another form of xenophobia. It was a narrative used by westerners to invade, conquer, and colonize the East.

Black, yellow, red, brown, and white are constructs used and created by white people to retain their power and authority over people of color. Whiteness is a social paradigm fabricated to maintain the status quo. Hence, one is not born white; rather, one becomes white. In the same way, one is not born red but becomes red. These are labels placed on people by white society as a form of control, restraint, and domination.

Whiteness is an unconscious state as it is often invisible to white people, who have no recognition for how it participates in oppressing communities of color. It shapes how white people view themselves and others and gives advantage to white people as white cultural norms and practices go unnamed and unchallenged. However, whiteness is not invisible nor inconsequential to those oppressed by it.[20] People of color who are on the receiving end of whiteness and white privilege experience subjugation in all aspects and arenas of life. It was present during the building of a nation and prevails strongly today as it affects politics, laws, religion, education, and daily life.

2

THE PROBLEM OF WHITENESS

Whiteness is problematic as it creates false boundaries between "us" and "them" and establishes a powerful and a powerless class. Whiteness engages in genocide, war, indenturing, enslavement, and redlining to maintain its power and advance its privilege. Whiteness is institutionalized in our workplaces, society, and religion, and provides entitlement to white people to take up as much space as they want and lay claim to all the riches and blessings from God. They use their privilege to talk down to other people and diminish other cultures and histories as unimportant or even evil. Whiteness has ruined North America and will continue to destroy it if it is not named and checked.

Whiteness is not factual; it is not a race but a mere idea that is very dangerous. It needs to be eliminated from our society if we are to achieve any form of liberation and freedom for all groups of oppressed people of color. Whiteness exists in the form of everyday microaggressions toward people of color such as verbal, nonverbal, and environmental slights, snubs, or insults. I have been told in workplaces many times that people of color are the problem. Until we showed up, everything—and they emphasize *everything*—was wonderful and fine. With the presence of people of color, things started to break down, creating havoc. The impact of microaggression is the feeling that you do not belong and that you are the other. I have experienced a devaluing of my Asian culture and have been treated as less than what the white culture offers to Americans.

When people ask me about my children and I tell them the good universities that they attended or are attending, they make snide remarks like "tiger mom," "you Asians are not oppressed," or "you Asians made it." These comments are hurtful because they dismiss all the racism and prejudice that we have experienced, as if it was imaginary. They reject the long history of discrimination that Asian Americans have experienced throughout our long immigrant story. I have met people who say, "Your English is so good!"—which basically connotes and assumes that as an Asian American I'm a perpetual foreigner. Another example of a microaggression is the frequent question I receive: "Where are you from?" If I answer Pennsylvania, they are never satisfied, and if I continue by saying Canada, they will ask, "Where are you *really* from?" These seemingly small acts leave us feeling frustrated, invisible, and marginalized.

Asian Americans have been blamed for the Covid-19 pandemic. We have been called names, and anti-Asian hate crimes have risen exponentially during this global health crisis. In response to the big surge in hate crimes against Asian American Pacific Islanders (AAPI) and the AAPI community, the organization Stop AAPI Hate was launched on March 19, 2020. From March 2020 to March 2022, over 11,500 racist incidents were reported. This number is just the tip of the iceberg; a national survey found that one in five Asian Americans experienced a hate incident in 2020 or 2021.[1] Since Asian Americans are not white, we are suspect for problems or diseases that spread in North America. As a result, we must always be mindful of our

Asianness and how it could be used against us and even be a death sentence for us.

Whiteness whitewashes an entire group of different people with different ethnicities, gathering them into a singular monolithic group as if their differences do not exist. This practice makes the "white group" appear pure while other groups are considered impure. People who are different from the white group are considered "ethnic," while the white group is not. Ethnic people belong to the different, less dominant and less favorable group. Such categories should be viewed and used with suspicion, as the powerful get to label and name others. This happens to me all the time because people do not recognize the diversity of Asia and just call me Chinese.

We often think of white supremacy as the Ku Klux Klan and racist attacks on African Americans, but white supremacist abuse is visited on all people of color. I was heading home from speaking at the Presbyterian Church in Canada, Synod of British Columbia, meeting when an incident on the plane ended a rather wonderful and fruitful trip on a sour note.[2] My daughter Elisabeth, who was eleven years old at that time, and I had to get up at 5:00 a.m. for a long trip back home from Vancouver. We left around 7:00 a.m., transferred in Dallas, and did not arrive in Philadelphia until around 9:00 p.m., and then we had to drive another hour to get home.

On the flight from Dallas to Philadelphia, I was seated in the second to last row with Elisabeth. An elderly white couple was seated behind us in the last row of the plane. When it came time to disembark, we rose at our appointed time to make our way down the aisle. This, of course, is an established system, and everyone has to wait their turn.

As we got up from our seats and stood in place to enter the aisle, the white woman behind me pushed into the aisle next to me and was determined to get ahead of me. Elisabeth was standing on the other side of me, and the woman's husband was standing behind her in the aisle. We stood a long time, as it seemed to take longer than usual for the passengers ahead of us to file out of the cabin. When it came closer to time for our row to exit, the elderly white woman behind me started walking ahead and somehow got three rows in front of us. I am not sure how she managed that, but she pushed ahead, leaving her husband behind us. This I could have attributed to simple rudeness.

As people were leaving the plane, I saw she was about eighteen passengers ahead of me on the ramp, and I asked her husband if he wanted to go ahead of us. He politely said, "Please go ahead." As my daughter and I emerged from the door of the plane ahead of her husband, the woman was waiting in disgust on the jet bridge for her husband. Her displeasure was written on her face, and as we walked past her, she said aloud to her husband, "I can't believe you allowed the Chinese to get ahead of you!"

She said it loud enough so I could hear. As the words left her mouth, her spiteful statement to her husband angered me more than such events may warrant. But her behavior was more than thoughtlessness or rudeness. Thoughtlessness is based on oversight. Rudeness is asserting oneself in a situation just to feel a momentary state of power over another. This case was more hurtful in that it invoked the notion that she was fundamentally better than us.

My first thought was the perception that an Asian is always viewed as a foreigner no matter how long he or she has been living in this country. Even fourth or fifth generation Asian Americans are viewed as the perpetual foreigner. Asian Americans are continuously portrayed as "unassimilable" and other stereotypes that continue to perpetuate racism and discrimination toward them, which is ongoing and persistent. Nearly every Asian American has been asked at some point, "Where are you *really* from?" The underlying assumption behind this "really" question is that Asian Americans cannot be "real" Americans like white people.[3] Instead, they are assumed to be foreigners. This is where we get the term *perpetual foreigners*, as it doesn't matter how many generations you have been here in the United States because Asian Americans will continue to be viewed as a foreigner or a stranger. In contrast, white Americans, even if they are descendants of first-generation immigrants, are "true" Americans. They may be unable to speak English or speak it with a French, Scottish, or Italian accent, but they are still accepted as Americans and their accents are welcomed, respected, and even regarded as "beautiful and intelligent" while Asian accents are devalued and laughed at. All of this marginalizes, otherizes, and causes much hurt to Asian Americans. Asian Americans carry the pain with us even though others may not see or recognize it as society makes our concerns, issues, and oppression invisible.

My second thought in this racist encounter was that it wasn't so much that she didn't allow for the possibility that I was Korean (or Vietnamese or Thai or Mongol or Tibetan or Japanese) and not Chinese. It was her tone and false understanding of Asians in general. In her mind, white people cannot allow Asians to get ahead of them in any aspect of their lives. At many times and in many places, I have felt that communities around me fabricate a glass ceiling that prevents Asians from getting ahead or moving up the social, economic, and political ladder. We are viewed as good but not good enough to be at the top.

Somehow, those of us who do not have a specific set of physical features are regarded as secondary human beings. As long as our social position mimics our role, it would seem there are no problems. However, once some see us as moving beyond that secondary station or achieving more than our subordinate status dictates, we are ignored, blamed, and made the other. One's Asianness signifies to the white-dominant group that they are a foreigner. This is true regardless of how many generations of their family have been residents of this country. It is this racial difference, this physical difference of appearance, that marks Asian Americans as other, creating the status of perpetual foreigner, and functions to permanently marginalize Americans of Asian descent. For women, it is even more complex: they have to endure both the patriarchal attitudes of their Asian ethnicity and those of their US context.[4]

My experience on that plane was precisely rooted in white privilege, which gave the white woman permission to believe that she has every right to discriminate and to believe that she can get away with it.

This plane incident was additionally distressing to me because I did not experience it alone. My young daughter also had to experience firsthand the humiliation of being attacked based on our skin color. I am not sure why the disposition to demean some other people based on racial background still exists and permeates much of our society. The ignorance or lack of respect for people with differences becomes visible in so many aspects of our lives. However, we need to move beyond the color of our skin or the size of our eyes or noses. We need to celebrate overcoming the evil influence created by a viral perception of differences that are before us rather than being fixated on them and allowing them to come between people.

I envision a world for my daughter in which people of all races, ethnicities, sexual orientations, and social classes can come together in harmony and love. My daughter's world should be free of hatred, racism, sexism, and other "isms." Each one of us can work toward it and try to help it happen. But how do we do that?

WHAT TO DO ABOUT WHITE SUPREMACY

The United States became perceived as a white country early in its formation, and this has had implications on religion and society. Unpacking American white identity, white privilege, and white supremacy will help us understand race relations, the roots of hate crimes, and the racialization of people of color.

White supremacy is the false belief that whites are the best and are superior over people of color. We are all taught to accept this lie, which leads to unjust social structures that exist to benefit white people.

For three centuries before the civil rights movement, white supremacy spread based on this presumption, and it became the dominant ideology to keep people of different ethnicities in line. This lie spread to other parts of the world enabling colonialism and imperialism in Africa, South America, and Asia. The notion of white superior identity spread to the detriment of people of color around the globe. There were plenty of dissenters, such as Dr. Martin Luther King Jr. and Nelson Mandela, who made their mark and whose influence is continuously felt today.

The idea of white supremacy predates the word *racism* to describe a system of interlocking racial privileges by eighty years. White supremacy was reserved for the most shocking examples of racism, suggesting radical violence in the form of cross burnings and lynchings.[5] However, white supremacy isn't so blatant; it is deceptive in how it infiltrates and exists in society, work, church, and neighborhoods. White supremacy is as damaging and ruthless today as it was in the past, but we now understand that it shows up in subtle ways as laws and norms that maintain disparities of wealth, education, housing, incarceration, and political power.

White supremacy dismembers, separates, and eliminates the memory and history of peoples of European descent, allowing them to forget who they really are and their own histories of oppression and degradation in Europe, ignoring why and how they came to this land. But memory is important as it serves as a roadmap to move us forward. We need to know and remember our past so we will not forget who we are. In Scripture, God tells the Hebrews to remember that they were once enslaved in Egypt. Their remembrance of the past serves to remind them that God is the source of their liberation, which will serve as a source of humility to move forward into the future. White people must remember their past and see how whiteness elevated them economically and legitimized the use of enslaved Africans. Those with power will do anything to retain it and preserve it for future generations, including war, genocide, and legislation.[6]

White supremacy ensures discriminatory access to education and jobs for less qualified white people.[7] Many do not see this selective protection happening right before their eyes, as people of color have to work exponentially harder to get the same recognition and compensation as a white male coworker who is less productive, less qualified, and less effective.

WHITE CULTURE AND ME

The white-dominant culture conveys a superiority complex that affects nonwhites in every aspect of their everyday lives—while shopping, pursuing activities, or performing tasks at work—and we are made to feel like second-class citizens. No matter what we do or how much we succeed, our level of excellence is always perceived as less than that of the white man. Even the mediocre achievements of a white man are weighted as greater than any excellent contributions and success from women of color. This is how whiteness works, and it is destructive to communities and people of color.

When I visit Korea or any other country in Asia, I encounter people who perceive America as a nation of white people rather than as a multiracial/multiethnic country. Many don't realize or recognize that Native Americans have lived here for thousands of years before Europeans set foot on this precious land. This misconception has led people to misunderstand the national identity of North Americans, believing them to be white and failing to understand the evil of whiteness in American history.

Connected to whiteness is white privilege—white people holding political, institutional, and economic power and receiving advantages that nonwhite groups do not. White people may experience marginalization due to gender or sexual identity, but not for race.[8] But since race weighs heavily in how one is perceived and welcomed in society, it can have an overbearing impact on people of color. Race is visible, so prejudice and oppression can happen within seconds of meeting or encountering someone. White people carry their privilege when they apply for jobs, board airplanes, drive cars, work, and navigate all other aspects of life.

White superiority is the presumption, and white privilege is the material consequence. We need to renegotiate justice by making this privilege visible to everyone and dismantling it. This begins by acknowledging that we have assigned such tremendous significance to race, both historically and today, and that it provides unearned advantages to those racialized white, albeit to varying degrees. This is not natural and only perpetuates oppression of people of color. Race is not a social category that stands alone, but rather a dynamic interaction with gender, sexuality, and class.[9]

In order to fight against white privilege, we must recognize that it is deeply embedded in our culture and society. The white woman on the plane sincerely believed that Asians are people who cannot and should not "get ahead" of white people. In fact, white privilege is entrenched so profoundly in the life of Americans that white people don't even recognize their own privilege. They are born into this white privilege, and since it grants them access to restricted benefits, they have no reason to question or acknowledge their own skin-ordained privilege. These benefits and privileges are carefully guarded from people of color.

White-dominant culture and society works as an organic social mechanism that creates endless privileges and advantages to white people. One enormous advantage is that they do not necessarily have to think about their racial identity, because whiteness is normalized,[10] while the rest of us have to think about it, and at times our racial identity determines our actions, behaviors, and mannerisms. In such a reality, white people seeking redemption need to decolonize their own lives wherever and whenever they can. It is through understanding how race was developed that we can make sense of our present racist culture.

The racialization of people of color did not occur in isolation. The concepts of whiteness and Christianity are not mutually exclusive of each other. Rather, they feed off each other with Christianity legitimizing whiteness and whiteness enabling Christianity to uphold white superiority and privilege. Christianity became a tool to reinforce white supremacy and white privilege. And, in turn, whiteness maintained a white Christian religion. Next we will look at how Christianity became white and continues to reinforce racism, discrimination, and oppression of people of color.

3

BECOMING A WHITE CHRISTIANITY

One of the most interesting trips in my life was a visit to Turkey with my oldest son when he was eight years old. It was a tremendously hot summer when we traveled with the Lehigh Dialogue Center to engage in Christian-Muslim dialogue. During our trip we visited several cities such as Istanbul, Izmir, Ephesus, and Cappadocia. In Cappadocia we visited rows and rows of rock formations that stood like giant pillars of brown salt. There were hundreds of these rock pillars scattered all over the land, as if some giant poured gravel over the place for fun. I later found out that these tall and stunning rock formations were created from ancient volcanic eruptions that had blanketed the region with ash that later solidified into a soft rock structure.

My son and I couldn't wait to get off the tour bus to climb up one of these rock pillars. He was a quick climber and raced ahead of me, yelling, "Climb up, Mom!" He exclaimed that there were caves inside the pillars. I strutted along as quickly as I could under the blistering summer sun to scale the rock formation. Once I caught up to him, we went into a cave and found cool temporary shelter from the pounding hot sun. As we entered the small cave, we saw what looked like a tiny home. There was a flat rock surface that looked like it could have been someone's bed and a small rock at the end of it that may have served as a pillow. The tour guide explained that early Christians who were persecuted hid in these strange stone caves, fearing for their lives. Some of these caves were a bit larger and served as places of worship.

After exploring the stone pillars, we went to see an underground city that offered further refuge from the heat. I was astounded as we wound our way down many steps into the ground where we found long underground tunnels that led to different homes, meeting places, and even churches. It was an amazing pathway of tunnels that served as a haven for persecuted Christians. These Christians even built hideaways and positioned rollaway stones that could block tunnel paths if they were ever invaded by persecutors. The underground city was built during the eighth and seventh centuries BCE by the Phrygians, and now there are two hundred cities in total. Christians during the Byzantine era continued to build and appropriate these underground cities to protect themselves from persecution. The high level of intricacy and security that went into planning the underground cities for people is incredible and fascinating to me. It was truly valuable to me to see evidence of the persecution early Christians faced and where the history of my faith originated. It was not lost on me how the tables have surely turned in who holds the upper hand now.

The first thing I noticed while visiting Egypt when I attended the COP27 meeting in Sharm el-Sheikh was that the people have dark skin. They are not light skinned as European whites, but are darker like Qataris and Saudi Arabians. I mention this observation because it only occurred to me during this visit how blatantly racist the teachings of the modern Christian church are. If you were raised in the Christian faith, you may have heard much of the history of when and where Jesus lived and still have missed some important insights. One of the most egregious misconceptions perpetuated relates to Jesus' ethnicity.

For Jesus and his family to flee to Egypt in order to escape genocide, it would have been essential for them to blend in with the rest of the Egyptians. They wanted to live in Egypt and be undetected. Jesus being dark-skinned meant that he could do this. Had he been light skinned with blond hair and light blue eyes, as depicted in European Christianity, he would have stood out like a sore thumb. Born as a dark-skinned man, Jesus was later transformed into a European man in the image of the ruling Roman emperors of his time.

Christianity emerged as a religion arising from the teachings of Jesus—a dark-skinned Jewish teacher who healed the sick, shared the good news, fed the hungry, and clothed the naked. He had many followers, and after his crucifixion and resurrection, his disciples decided to share his good news with others as far as they could reach. Jesus' followers went to different parts of Asia Minor to share the gospel and formed house churches throughout. It was through these house churches that the message of Jesus was shared and spread. As the influence of Christianity widened, the early church members started to face persecution due to their faith, beginning in 64 CE under Emperor Nero through 311 CE in the East and up to 313 CE in the West.

THE BIRTHING OF A FAITH

Now let's look at the history and put it into context. Christianity was born in the Middle East in Palestine under the Roman Empire around two thousand years ago. The Roman Empire controlled this area heavily, and controlled its territories in different ways. In the East (eastern Asia Minor, Syria, Palestine, and Egypt), territories were governed by kings who were puppet kings for the

Roman Empire and did whatever the empire wished. During the time of Jesus, Jewish Palestine and some of the neighboring Gentile areas were ruled by Herod the Great. Palestine was strategic for Rome because it was between Syria and Egypt, which were valuable countries to Rome. Roman imperial policy required that Palestine be loyal and peaceful so that it did not undermine Rome's larger interests. This was achieved by permitting Herod to remain king of Judea (37–4 BCE) and allowing him to freely govern his kingdom, as long as he achieved the requirements of stability and loyalty.[1] Palestinians were olive-complexioned people who lived under the burden of the Roman Empire that taxed them heavily. It was under the reign of King Herod that Jesus was born in Bethlehem. The three magi saw a bright star in the heavens and went in search of the newborn king who was Jesus. They told Herod that a new king was born and, upon hearing this, Herod grew very jealous. As a result, he commanded all boys under two years old living in the vicinity of Bethlehem to be killed. This is why Mary and Joseph took baby Jesus and fled to Egypt to protect him from the genocide that Herod unleashed. They lived in Egypt till Herod passed away (see Matthew 2:16-18).

The change in rulership changed everything. Christianity became the official religion of the Roman Empire in 313 CE under Emperor Constantine I (c. 280–337 CE). He was the first Christian emperor and issued the Edict of Milan, which legalized Christian worship. The impact this edict had on Christianity cannot be overstated, as it was now an acceptable religion in the Roman Empire, and Christians did not have to face persecution from ruling authorities.

Typically, leaders who want to keep an empire unified seek to keep people under one religion with the same beliefs and practices. This keeps people uniform without too many differences that could lead to conflict. As such, Christianity became the predominant Roman religion in the state church of the Roman Empire.

During that same trip to Turkey with my son, we also visited the wondrous Hagia Sophia. The outside structure appears massive and grand, but inside the Hagia, the main area is simply an open space that felt much smaller than I expected. Walking around the Hagia Sophia and admiring the grand building, I felt a bit torn and disappointed. The Hagia was first built as a church, then it became a mosque, and now is a museum. For me, it seemed that the holiness within this sacred space was diminished by making it into a museum. But with tensions arising between Christians and Muslims, who both laid claim to the place of worship, the best option was to make it into a museum that would be open to everyone.

My son was a bit too young to understand the importance of this visit, but I was deeply grateful that I was able to visit the Hagia. As we walked through the upper floors and saw the artwork and pictures of prominent visitors to the Hagia, I got a warm sense of the long history and all of the amazing people who have worshiped and walked through this majestic place. The Hagia makes a deep and lasting impression on you.

This building represents compromise among shared history and shared culture, but we haven't always navigated that well. In fact, an astonishing amount of war is waged over who has the right take on religion and, even more specifically, Christianity and who Jesus was.

BUILDING A CHRISTIAN EMPIRE

During the Middle Ages (fifth to fifteenth centuries), Christianity spread west to Germany under the Byzantine empire. During the High Middle Ages, Eastern and Western Christianity grew apart, which led to the East-West Schism in 1054. Then, as people of faith witnessed inconsistencies and problems within the Roman Catholic Church, the Protestant Reformation occurred in the sixteenth century to protest some of the Roman Catholic teachings. During the time of the Renaissance (fourteenth to seventeenth centuries), Christianity started to spread throughout the rest of the developing world. Colonialism and imperialism were part of the mix of spreading Christianity. There are now more than two billion Christians across the globe, and it has become the world's largest religion.

Empire building still happens today. In our current political climate, we see a strong American empire trying to rally its people together. When President George W. Bush tried to rally Americans to come together after 9/11—which was a rallying call under the disguise of a white American Christian empire—his message was a strong urging to stick together and fight the evil penetrating our borders: the dark-skinned Muslims. When Bush was trying to convince Congress and American citizens of the need to invade Iraq, he called the invasion a "holy war," hoping it would help legitimize his war plans. Bush shared his religious fervor when he spoke at Sharm e-Sheikh, four months after the US-led invasion of Iraq in 2003. One of the delegates, Nabil Shaath, said, "President Bush said to all of us: 'I am driven with a mission from God. God would tell me, *George, go and fight these terrorists in Afghanistan.* And I did. And then God would tell me, *George, go and end the tyranny in Iraq.* And I did.'"[2] Bush referenced crusades and described the invasion as a war against terrorism, against his better judgment, as he recalled the wars against Arabs and Muslims in the eleventh, twelfth, and thirteenth centuries. It was Augustine who developed the just-war theory in the fifteenth century based on the understanding that there are worse evils than physical destruction. This just-war theory has been a dominant Christian empire-building position used repeatedly since Augustine's time to wage wars and crusades.

WHITE CHRISTIAN HISTORY

The church was born and bred within a Greco-Roman philosophy, culture, and empire. Although Christianity emerged in Palestine—which is not part of Europe—the fact that Palestine was under the Roman Empire meant that Roman philosophy, culture, and practices influenced and formed Christianity. Christianity did not emerge in Palestine as a white religion, but it eventually became a white (Eurocentric) religion and continues to be white dominated today.

Eurocentric Christianity has done significant harm around the world. Since the days of Constantine, Eurocentric Christianity has defended authoritarian regimes, such as emperors, kings, crusading popes, and military dictators. White European Christianity has been used by rulers to sustain and maintain their power. In the last century, Eurocentric Christian messages tolerated and sustained evil regimes, which had carried on inconceivable violations against humanity. One example is the Catholic Church, who was afraid of losing power during Spain's Second Republic (1931–1939), supporting the right-wing politics of Francisco Franco (1939–1975). Franco covered himself as a true defender of religious liberties, but he committed terrible atrocities. He used forced labor and had concentration camps and executions causing thirty thousand to fifty thousand deaths. Franco declared that Catholicism was the only religion to be tolerated but used this as a way to commit deaths and hide his evil actions.[3]

Conquest. The history of white Christianity is littered with wars waged on those who are seen as other. Leaders have justified conquering groups of people by turning the lens of Christianity on a culture to invalidate its existence. Conquests were central to the expansion of white European theology. Christians felt that it was all right to conquer and wipe away those who were not yet Christians. Non-Christians were seen as evil heathens in need of salvation. In the pursuit of conquering land and people throughout the Enlightenment period, European Christians were actually wrestling with God for control and dominion over the planet. For a time, whites won. The prize was control, status, and an expanding empire; Black, Native, and Brown bodies were collateral damage in a war waged against God. Under the legal shelter of Pope Nicholas V's Romanus Pontifex,[4] Christians went to conquer lands, destroying people of color and indigenous peoples in the process. Some of the effects of colonialism will never be reversed, as the outrageous harm is irreversible.

Colonialism. My grandmother, born in 1911, grew up during Japanese colonialism, and it affected her entire life. I remember her telling me stories of what happened to her and other young people. When she was in school, she had to change her Korean name to a Japanese name. Our names are tied to our identities as Korean names carry family and ancestral identity, and each name is associated with thoughtful meanings and aspirations. There are usually three characters in a Korean name. It begins with the family name followed by two characters, one of which is called *dol-rim*. *Dol-rim* is the character used by all the cousins in the same generation on the father's side of the family. Hence, it becomes easy to identify the generation that you are born in, in case you find long-lost relatives or distant family members. Addressing people by the correct name/address is important in Korea. For example, I met a distant older man (my father's age) in my church. But through our *dol-rim*, he said that I am in the older generation and called me auntie, regardless of me being much younger than him. Therefore, taking on Japanese names during Japanese colonialism led to the sense of loss of Korean identity. Koreans were actually forced to take on a

Japanese identity, which is devastating and consequential. My grandmother was also taught Japanese history, culture, and language in school in lieu of learning her own Korean history and culture. This was a means by the Japanese of asserting control over those they sought to subjugate.

As a child, I went to revival services to hear guest speakers from Korea. I recall one elderly woman relating her time under Japanese colonialism. She described the threats Korean Christians faced if they did not denounce their faith. The Japanese soldiers would round up Christians and place them in a line. They'd throw a Bible onto the ground and insist each Korean Christian step on it as a way to publicly denounce their faith. She said it was a very difficult thing. When people didn't step on the Bible, they were pushed to the ground and beaten.

Colonialism is a nice way of labeling the conquest and control of other people's land, bodies, natural resources, and goods. Many colonialists used women's bodies for their own sexual pleasure and dominance. Women were seen as only being useful for domestic work, child rearing, and cheap labor. Colonialism is not merely the expansion of various European powers into Asia, Africa, or the Americas; it has been a widespread feature of human history.[5] We see powerful nations colonizing other countries and taking their resources, land, and people for economical gain.

White Christianity and missiology are intertwined with colonialism, and it has had devastating effects all over the world. Whiteness is the root of much colonialism around the globe, and there are four deadly weapons employed in white Christian conquests: genocide, enslavement, removal, and rape. These weapons divide people, separating them from land, people, story, culture, and identity. These weapons serve colonizers in gaining more land and low-cost or no-cost labor to grow wealth.[6]

CONSEQUENCES OF COLONIALISM

Colonialism was not applied or executed equally around the world, but in every case it locked the Native inhabitants and the newcomers into a complex and traumatic relationship. Colonialists unformed and reformed the communities that existed already through trade, plunder, warfare, genocide, enslavement, and rebellions.[7] Europeans traveled in all directions, in search of wealth and power, to colonize people. They viewed Natives as primitive and those from the East as degenerate and inferior to those from the West.

The death toll of the colonization project from 1493 to 1899 is estimated to be around fifty million, about 90 percent of the Native American population. In the twentieth century one colonized nation after another fought to be liberated from colonial domination. The "civilized" Christian West fought to maintain colonial dominance as long as it possibly could as it benefited them financially, politically, and religiously.[8] The brutality and the enormous force used against Natives is unfathomable. The sheer acceptance of white Christians' acts of violence against Natives as legitimate and acceptable is hard to swallow. Especially if the key message of Christianity is to "love your neighbor."

Possibly the most lasting negative impact of colonization was fragmentation of the conquered. Four generations after conquest, names of family members were often lost or destroyed. Family and community stories were forgotten, forbidden, twisted, or hidden as the colonized were forced to rehearse and remember their new identity, which was usually tied to the colonizers. To enforce colonialism, subsequent generations were often educated apart from their parents and communities. They were taught their people's story from the distorted point of view of the settlers in schools with curricula established by those settlers.[9]

When Japan annexed Korea from 1910 to 1945, they attempted to erase Korean culture, history, and language. Even the country name Korea was officially changed to Chosen, and this name was recognized internationally until the end of the Japanese occupation. Korean politics and economy were integrated with Japan as Japan set up a government in Korea. Korea was filled with Japanese generals or admirals who were appointed by the Japanese emperor. Japanese civilians also moved to Korea and took over Korean land and resources.

Beginning in 1932 through WWII (1939–1945), young Korean women were kidnapped or taken by Japanese soldiers under the pretense of being offered a factory job; these women, known as *comfort women*, were forced to work as sexual slaves in various Japanese military stations in Asia. They were locked up in small rooms where they were raped by fifty to seventy Japanese soldiers a day. This was brutal physical and mental torture of these young Korean girls and women by the Japanese government and military.

When I was a college student, an elderly Korean comfort woman survivor came to Toronto to give a public talk about her experience under the Japanese military. I went to this event without knowing much about comfort women and listened with devastation and heartache as the survivor recounted her daily life of existence. When she was first taken to a military station someplace in Asia, she was put into a tiny room. A high-ranking general came in and beat her, and then he raped her brutally. She was so terrified by the Japanese general that she eventually passed out in fear. When she woke, there was blood all over her clothes and the thin mattress on the floor. As a young girl, she feared for her life and could not comprehend what had actually happened to her.

Then lower ranking soldiers lined up outside her room waiting to rape her. At the end of the day, she could barely walk or move because she was in tremendous pain. I cried so much listening to her painful and horrific story, unable to imagine such horrific acts committed against my people. Many Korean comfort women contracted venereal diseases and were often executed as useless if they didn't die from the disease itself. They were taken outside naked in front of the other comfort women. The soldiers then would put a gun up their vagina and shoot them dead. Their limp, violated bodies were then thrown into the dumpster for every comfort woman to witness. It was a fear tactic used against the women so that they would not run away or try anything against the raping soldiers.

The few comfort women survivors, like the one who gave the talk in Toronto, were set free when the Japanese were defeated during WWII. Some comfort women returned home to Korea to live alone in poverty, too ashamed to return to their families and unable to marry due to their horrific past as sexual slaves. It was a life of shame, broken bodies, and misery. To this day the Japanese government has not acknowledged its role in the devastating actions against these comfort women and has not compensated them for being subjected to sexual slavery. Even though time has passed, these negative aspects of colonization are still felt today in modern Korea and will continue to last for generations.

Additionally, many young Korean girls and women were forced into prostitution to service American soldiers for decades during and after the Korean War. These prostitution rings were run by pimps and even facilitated by the Korean government. During the Korean War, they were known as the "special comfort women units" for South Korean soldiers, and "comfort stations" for American-led UN troops. After the war, many of these young Korean girls and women ended up working in *gijichon* or "camp towns," which were purposely created around American military bases so that they could sexually service the American soldiers.[10] Many of the surviving women feel wronged and betrayed by their country as the Korean government encouraged prostitution to maintain its military alliance with the United States and to gain American dollars used to pay for the services.

Some of these young women who were forced into prostitution endured harsh beatings and other forms of abuse from GIs. They also suffered venereal diseases, and the infected women were kept in facilities with barred windows and were administered heavy doses of penicillin, which is very dangerous. Some of these women collapsed or died from penicillin shock. Prostitution was and remains illegal in South Korea today, but these *gijichon* were created to confine these young women sex workers so that they could be easily monitored and controlled. They were also created and maintained to prevent prostitution and sex crimes involving American GIs from infiltrating the rest of Korean society. Some of these women were brutally assaulted and even viciously murdered by American soldiers.[11] These are some of the devastating realities of American colonial power in the name of military aid in Korea. The American soldiers assaulted and murdered young women whose bodies have not been recovered by their families due to the shame that they brought to their families. This is a tragedy that cannot be ignored as it arose to satisfy American military men and their power in Korea.

COLONIALISM IN INDIA, SOUTH AFRICA, AND THE CARIBBEAN

India has a long, devastating history of colonialism by various Europeans, including Austrians, Swedes, French, Dutch, Danish, and most notably the British Raj (1858–1947). Being colonized by the British led to many negative economic, religious, and political consequences, such as the restriction of Indian industries, including its popular textile industry. Colonialism also led to the rise of cash crops, which resulted in the loss of self-sufficiency for many villagers. The British colonialization led to the British empire taking goods and resources from India to profit and enrich themselves. Further, British colonizers enforced a system of racial and cultural inferiority. When the British finally left in 1947, the subcontinent was divided into Muslim majority Pakistan and Hindu majority India.

Other places around the world were also colonialized by Europeans. South Africa was first colonized by the Netherlands (1652–1795 and 1803–1806) and by Great Britain (1795–1803 and 1801–1961), which had enormous repercussions on its people and its land. The European colonizers made Africans produce goods for export and not for use by their local people. This led the Africans to abandon production of their own food items for their own sustainability. Colonialism profits the colonizers, and at times, it can be disguised as economic growth for the colonized. But this all comes at the expense of the Native peoples as their political independence is replaced with foreign rules. Furthermore, the imposition of white European culture on Africans without any respect for their own culture resulted in loss and disenfranchisement. European Christianity was transported to Africa without any respect for African religions, spirituality, culture, and their rich religious history.

The Caribbean also struggled with European colonialism beginning in the fifteenth century as Christopher Columbus landed in the Caribbean in 1492 and claimed the area for Spain. The next year the first Spanish settlers arrived in the Caribbean. Non-Hispanic traders and settlers established colonies and trading posts on the islands. They started a system of sugar planting, which led to a system of enslavement. These islands were already inhabited by different indigenous groups before the Spanish, English, Dutch, and French colonizers arrived. Portugal, Sweden, and Denmark also held possession of various Caribbean islands. Colonialism in the Caribbean resulted in the death of many indigenous peoples as well as the enslavement of Africans.

Colonialism is highly problematic as it depletes the natural resources of the colonized to enrich the colonizers. There is no benefit to the colonized as they lose identity, wealth, and their own cultural and historical ways of being. Being colonized is traumatizing, and the colonized suffer poverty, disease, cultural displacement, economic exploitation, depletion of natural resources, and political uneasiness. But for the white Europeans who went to many places around the globe, colonization was a way to line their own pockets.

Colonizers employed the process of "othering" to reduce Natives to being backward and inferior while viewing themselves as good and progressive. The colonized were treated as lazy, aggressive, violent, greedy, sexually promiscuous, and irrational. This othering of the colonized made it easier for the colonizers to take over their lands, their resources, and the people.

Even before all these atrocious acts of enslavement and colonial plunder toward Africans began, racist stereotypes and prejudices were already embedded in society. Racial stereotyping can be found in the Greek and Roman periods, setting the stage for European images and views of barbarians and outsiders. These negative views were reworked in medieval and early modern Europe by Christians. To justify their mistreatment of savages and outsiders, they conveniently associated dark-skinned peoples with the descendants of Ham and the concept of evil.[12] Even though Genesis 9 never says that Ham was dark-skinned, there was a folk etymology from his name that was connected to the word for "dark" or "brown." This unfortunate narrative gave an excuse for superiority of one ethnic group over another. The (dark-skinned) Natives needed to be brought back into the good fold, and the white colonizers were the only ones who could do that.

THE DOCTRINE OF DISCOVERY

Immigration has existed as long as humans have. People move in search of greener pastures for farming and hunting, better climates, and other improvements to their quality of life. Movement has been part of human living and survival. White European immigrants are the ones who brought Christianity to various parts of the world, but particularly to the United States and Canada. Unfortunately, they used Christianity against Native Americans and people of color for personal and economic gain.

A series of teachings from Christian colonizers led to catastrophe for Native peoples around the world. The first of these was a *papal bull*, or public decree, from Pope Nicholas V in 1492 that gave Christians the permission to call people pagans (among other names) if they did not profess Christian beliefs. This teaching, which led to land theft by Christians around the world, is called the Doctrine of Discovery. This Doctrine of Discovery has been strategically hidden in our church history, as the average church member or minister would not know about it. The Doctrine of Discovery served as the legal basis for the conquest of indigenous lands.[13] Since the church endorsed it, people believed that it was an act and a will of God.

The Doctrine of Discovery was a set of legal principles in the fifteenth and sixteenth centuries that shaped European colonizers in their taking over and use of indigenous land. Even though centuries have passed, it is still the main legal practice that controls Native affairs and rights. But it is all based on a distorted theology that pushed and validated European colonial settler worldview and perspective.[14] The Doctrine of Discovery affirmed European imperial ambitions and gave theological permission for Europeans to view themselves as superior to non-Europeans. This doctrine generated an outsider identity for non-Europeans. For example, it deemed Africans as inferior and determined who can be subjected to subjugation. It also relegated the original inhabitants of the land "discovered" to outsiders and even unwelcomed in their own land.[15]

The Doctrine of Discovery had immense consequences for the Natives who already lived on the land. Millions of indigenous people around the world have suffered genocide, land theft, cultural humiliation, displacement, and apartheid. These atrocious acts have long-lasting negative effects that get passed on from one generation to the next. Today many feel disenfranchised and disillusioned, and desire to gain their land, culture, and history back.

As colonists arrived in the land that would become the United States, the territory was considered empty because indigenous people were not Christians and therefore not human and nonexistent. As such, you can do what you want to the land and to the indigenous people. For centuries, a white nation was built on stolen land and white people never admitted their acts of theft because they were sanctioned by the church through whiteness. White people today believe themselves to be self-made rich and prosperous through their own hard work, and they preach to people of color to do the same. Meanwhile, they are ignorant of how their own wealth and land originated and do not understand that it only exists because of all they took from Native communities and communities of color.[16] Historical amnesia is deadly because history will repeat itself over and over again if not remembered. This is why we must teach our young people the truth about white American history of colonialism, theft of land, domination, and genocide. They will only do better by knowing better. The narrative of the American dream mistakenly suggests that by working hard and being diligent, every American citizen will have an equal opportunity to achieve success, wealth, and prosperity. But this narrative fails to recognize white people's path to wealth and also how racism creates an uneven playing field and blocks opportunities for people of color.

Roxanne Dunbar-Ortiz states, "Everything in US history is about the land—who oversaw and cultivated it, fished its waters, maintained its wildlife, who invaded and stole it; how it became a commodity (real estate) broken into pieces to be bought and sold on the market."[17] This is the history of North America that is not frequently told or shared. Now many white people just want to ignore it, forget it, and wipe it from their history.

The Doctrine of Discovery and whiteness were used to eliminate Native Americans from their own land, and then attempted to erase this genocide from American history. As a result, indigenous culture has become foreign and unknown to so many Americans. Native American culture is often seen as either exotic or threatening, especially within educational systems, politics, and the church.[18] Indigenous culture has been eliminated from curriculum and not taught in our educational systems or in our society as a whole. Often indigenous culture is viewed as a sports mascot or a cute Halloween costume with no respect and honor to the historical customs and spiritualities. Many white Americans fail to remember their own participation in this mass genocide and erasure of a people, their identity, history, culture, and spirituality.

White European Christian settler colonialists who stole the land had to legitimize the claim that was needed to make them superior over the indigenous people. The thieves who stole the land decided to hold power over those who originally held the land by creating dysfunctional narratives that elevated their own dominant sense of worth. This lie of supremacy created and reinforced by the dominant group was used to define the other as less than and proclaimed power over them.[19] White Americans legitimized their power and takeover of the indigenous lands. This was a religious as well as a social legitimation that was orchestrated to take over the land.

The Christian church not only legitimized the taking of land from indigenous people but also dominated them and pushed them to assimilate into white culture and religion. Indigenous people were pressured into rejecting their own beautiful indigenous heritage and culture. Children were separated from families and put into Christian boarding schools. Natives had to burn their traditional clothes and not engage in any of their "evil" traditional songs or dances.

It is deeply problematic that the church has been so complicit in Native people's struggles in the past and today.[20] We cannot have any form of reconciliation unless the church repents and acknowledges its historical actions and sins. Native Americans have suffered too much, having lost their land, their lives, their families, and their livelihood stemming from the Doctrine of Discovery. Reconciliation cannot happen until both sides come in harmony to accept (reconcile) the past as it truly happened, not the whitewashed version.

Some denominations are wanting to take down the Doctrine of Discovery or revoke it in attempts to move toward reconciliation. The Indigenous Water Protectors movement emerged in 2016 with the Standing Rock Sioux Tribe. This movement began due to their respect for water as taught by their own indigenous culture. The Water Protectors fought at Standing Rock Reservation against big corporate oil pipelines that were directly contaminating their drinking water supplies. Hundreds of clergy members came to Standing Rock in solidarity and even destroyed a copy of the Doctrine of Discovery to show how evil and unjust it was. Additionally, the Declaration of Independence is another problematic document. Some Christians strongly uphold this document even though it portrays indigenous people as "merciless Indian savages."[21]

If the church really wants to move toward reconciliation, it needs to recognize its own participation in sin and the destruction of indigenous peoples. White Christians need to learn about the rich culture and history of Native Americans and not disregard them as trivial and unimportant. Christians need to honor and respect indigenous traditions and carefully listen to their prayers, regalia, songs, sacred drumming, and dance. The white church must come to welcome and recognize indigenous peoples as a vital part of God's community and kin-dom on earth.

The church must repent and seek reconciliation for the injustices committed against all indigenous and othered peoples. Embracing a both/and approach to Christianity and faith will help the church move toward a more holistic view of faith and spirituality. Syncretism and mixing of religions and culture have always been part of the Christian church history, and we need to allow this syncretism to exist for every culture. No culture should have to deny its ancestral history and heritage to become a Christian.

Kaitlin Curtice, a member of the Potawatomi tribe, writes, "The word for America, *kchemokmanke,* translates loosely to 'white person with long knives,'"[22] referring to the Europeans who invaded their lands and butchered their people. Language describes where people have come from and what it means to be indigenous.

Languages carry stories, experiences, heritages, and history that can be passed on verbally and through the written word. Whiteness has tried to steal this, but preserving indigenous heritage to pass on to their children is an essential part of reclaiming their own beautiful identity that has been denied to so many peoples around the world.

Words form our thoughts and ideas. Therefore, words matter and will continue to matter. The church is complicit in the evil of whiteness that has led to such atrocious acts against people of color. Decolonization is a spiritual matter just as it is a physical, mental, social, and political one.[23] Hence, we need to decolonize Christianity from its whiteness if anything is to change. This is not an easy task, for those who benefit from whiteness will try to maintain it as long as they can.

4

A MISSIOLOGY OF WHITENESS

Growing up in Canada, I heard so many stories of white missionaries going to Korea, China, India, and Japan. The Presbyterian Church in particular sent many missionaries to Korea, and white Christians never failed to remind me of the fabulous mission work they did in Asia. They would often ask me if I was Korean or Chinese. When I said I was Korean, they would go on to talk about themselves, their uncle, or a friend who went to Korea as a missionary and spent their entire lives spreading the good news in Korea. They would tell me with such pride and excitement as if they were godsent to evangelize the poor, lazy, and evil Koreans. At times, their attitude of superiority made me feel uncomfortable, as if they were telling me that Korea only became "developed" because the white missionaries helped them.

My mother took my sister and me to visit Korea in 1982. We had been living in Canada for the past seven years, and my paternal grandmother missed us so much that she sent airplane tickets for us to come visit her. While in Korea, my mother attended a lot of churches and church gatherings. There, she heard that missionaries had told Korean Christians that small trinkets, dolls, figurines, wooden carvings, and the like could "hold or house evil spirits," and my mother believed they could be right.

When we returned to Canada after a long hot summer in Korea, my mother went into action. As soon as she entered our small two-bedroom apartment, she gathered all the small items that could possibly house evil spirits and threw them in the garbage. There was a particular small, wooden Korean ox carving that we had brought to Canada when we first immigrated. The unique little carving sat on top of our second-hand, out-of-tune piano, and I loved and cherished it. I used to look at it when I didn't want to practice piano. My mother didn't care that I was weeping when she grabbed the wooden carving and threw it into her trash bag. I was in shock that she threw it out.

We didn't have many material things in our apartment, but another item that I liked was a Korean souvenir doll dressed in *hanbok*—traditional Korean dress. She quickly grabbed that doll as if it was possessed and threw it into the trash. Within minutes, our apartment was cleansed of everything that could possibly house evil spirits, and I couldn't understand why. To this day, I look back on her reaction with a bit of resentment toward her for throwing away everything that I liked in our tiny apartment. At the same time, however, I feared as a child that perhaps she may be right about evil spirits.

White missionaries thought the traditional Korean religions like Buddhism and shamanism were evil and dangerous. They thought that Koreans worshiped evil spirits and needed to turn away from their traditional beliefs and worship the white male God. Reflecting on this, I realize that white missionaries had infiltrated our culture and held an inordinate amount of influence if they were able to convince us that even our innocent and precious possessions were evil. I still am shocked about how that came to be. The influence of white missionaries' beliefs on Koreans was tremendous, and Koreans welcomed white culture, white philosophy, and white Christianity. It almost seemed like a ticket out of poverty for many Koreans, if only they embraced whatever teachings the white missionaries brought to them.

THE HISTORY OF MISSION WORK IN ASIA

Crusades were one of the earliest ways in which white Christians propagated whiteness. They were religious wars and military expeditions that occurred during the medieval period (beginning in the late eleventh century) and were often initiated and supported by the Latin church. At times they were viewed as a "Christian" form of invasion of other lands and people. Some crusades occurred in the Holy Land (1095–1291) to recover what was taken by Islamic rule. They reversed centuries of influence after the Muslim wars of expansion by reclaiming control of the Holy Land, taking over pagan lands, and recapturing lost Christian territories.

There were both church-sanctioned crusades and actions by individual citizens who engaged in crusades.[1] These crusades formed a dreadful pattern of how Christians interacted with non-Christians. The behavior toward non-Christians was violent and included acts of war and invasion in the name of God.

The crusades ended around the fifteenth century, but some would argue that they lasted another five hundred years under an alias of white European Christian colonialism. By the sixteenth century they ended with the emergence of the Protestant Reformation and the decline of the papal authority.[2]

When white Western Christians meet non-Christians who are mostly nonwhite, they generally operate under the crusader mentality and see their neighbors as dangerous and immoral opponents in a holy conflict. They try to convert them, or they require them to submit to white people as representatives of a white, male God. As a result, non-Christians are subjugated to a second-class status and live subordinate to white people. This crusader mentality dangerously serves to validate white Christians' innate feeling of superiority over people of different ethnicities and those who are non-Christians. There is an intersectionality of oppression, and white Christians feel they can continue to subordinate nonwhites and non-Christians.

Christian crusaders reaped huge profits from dominating other people and their lands. Today, crusader colonial spirit continues to live on as white supremacy and white Christian nationalism. Many white Christians would be loath to think of themselves as white supremacists but would be proud to think of themselves as Christian supremacists. Hence, their whiteness is hidden to both others and themselves in their Christianity.[3] In their minds, there is no shame in viewing the Christian as superior to the heathen because the saving grace of God is supposed to elevate them and make them greater. This is where the self-deception takes hold.

Expanding to Asia. The first Catholic Jesuit missionaries went to Asia in the 1500s. Francis Xavier (1506–1552), a prominent Jesuit, first went to India in 1542 and arrived in Goa where he found the Portuguese Catholics were very cruel to the enslaved people. He tried to combat this cruelty by helping the poor and sick and encouraging people to live a good life. After seven years on the South India coast, Francis moved on to Ceylon (present-day Sri Lanka) and then sailed to Kagoshima, Japan, in 1549 before arriving in Hirado.[4] During Xavier's mission work, he was able to convert around two thousand Japanese people to Christianity. He had hoped to travel to China but fell ill and died at the age of forty-six.

The history of white American Protestant mission work in Asia is significant and sheds light into the missiology of whiteness. It started in 1812 when eight young missionaries went to India to convert Indians to Christianity. After a promising start to their missionary work, the missionaries saw a gradual decline in conversion and interest in the faith. In the early 1880s, many foreign mission organizations were facing a similar fate. Numerous religious and volunteer societies grew in early nineteenth-century America only to see participation decline later. Despite the disinterest, missionaries continued to be sent out into the field. White American missionaries increased from 934 in 1890 to 5,000 at the turn of the century, and to 12,000 by the end of the 1920s.[5] There was a sudden increased interest in missiology and the strong desire to spread white good news to the people in Asia over the span of forty years. The need to convert and dominate in Asia became a popular strategy for the white churches in North America and Europe. Perhaps the disinterest became an even bigger motivation than actually saving lost souls.

Whiteness was part of the white missionary's message when they went to Asia to share the good news of Jesus Christ. The message of whiteness and the good news were so intertwined that, at times, they became one. Asians generally accepted this white gospel without questioning it. This acceptance of a white Christian message is in part due to Orientalism, defined as a Western approach to the Orient that emphasizes, exaggerates, and distorts Asians negatively in relation to Europeans. This had significant implications for Asians and how the West perceived and treated the East. The quest to conquer, colonize, and subjugate others in the name of God intensified. They went under the guise of missions, but in many cases, it was for economic interests. They were in search of natural resources and invaded these countries and took what they wanted and needed.

Taking over Korea. The first white missionaries to arrive in Korea during the 1840s were French Catholics sent by the Paris Foreign Missions Society.[6] In the 1880s, Koreans were debating over the reform of Korea and examining whether they should stay a closed country or open up the country to foreigners. Up to 1880s, Korea was an isolated country from the rest of the world and was often referred to as the hermit kingdom. They didn't want people coming in or any Koreans leaving Korea.

White American Protestant missionaries went to Korea about fifty years after the Catholic missionaries arrived. Contrary to the popular belief that they made many economic and lifestyle sacrifices to do missions in Korea, they actually lived very comfortably. The white American Protestant missionaries built living communities that were like an oasis in a desert. They built Western homes and furnished them in the same way they did back home with imported furniture and appliances. They also imported Western foods rather than adapting their palate to eat Korean foods. They lived middle-class American lives in Korea and had their families with them. Visiting these separate compounds, it looked as if they weren't even living in Korea. It is difficult to imagine how the white missionaries could live this way when they were preaching a gospel message of liberation and love to Koreans who lived poorly and with little means. When Koreans were hired to work for missionaries, they were only paid five dollars a month in comparison to as much as a two-thousand-dollar-a-year salary for white Presbyterian missionaries who had children.[7] With such a large income and the low cost of living in Korea, these white American missionaries' lives were in stark contrast to how Koreans were living at that time. The huge discrepancy in salary and living conditions between white missionaries and Koreans created a desire for some Koreans to be like the white missionaries. They had wishes of becoming wealthy just like the white people who seemed to live very lavish and comfortable lives. Rather than "suffering" in foreign countries as they gave up the comforts of their

Western lifestyle to serve the poor, savage pagans, the white missionaries brought all the comforts of their home to Korea.

This also differs significantly from the French Catholic missionaries who arrived during Korea's seclusion policy and had to work secretly to avoid persecution and death.[8] They lived among the commoners and conformed to the lifestyle of locals, eating local foods and engaging in local customs. But this was not the narrative of white American missionaries in Korea.

Koreans started to attend church for various reasons. Some were impressed by the white American missionaries' houses, luxurious lifestyles, and conveniences, and desired it for themselves. Some Koreans believed that they could get connected with rich and influential foreigners if they were close to the Western missionaries as this will greatly help them get jobs or other gains. Some Koreans associated missionaries with climbing the socioeconomic ladder. Additionally, some were able to get food, medicine, and work when they went to church,[9] which they otherwise would not be able to have access to, making it very advantageous to go to church. But there were others who were simply drawn to the Christian gospel message of hope and a new religious spirituality, which was foreign to them. Koreans were genuinely seeking new religious ways of being.

The good and comfortable lifestyles of missionaries enticed poor Koreans to Christianity and created an opening to the closed nation. The reform groups in Korea were open to Western education and welcomed white missionaries and Western investments. The missionary efforts were multifaceted and included evangelism, education, and medicine,[10] all of which were attractive to the reform groups in Korea. Missionaries ended up building churches, schools, universities, and hospitals, many of which are still present today.

Korean Christians appreciated the fact that the Christian church was open to all people, at least in theory. This was different from their own traditional Confucianism, which was stratified and hierarchical. Under Confucianism, society was layered by ancestry and segregated by gender, class, and education. There were a lot of restrictions for women, who were viewed as second-class citizens. Furthermore, lower socioeconomic classes were viewed negatively under Confucianism. The Christian church, in contrast, welcomed and included women and people of all ranks in society, including outcast groups.[11] This was a fresh outlook and approach to society for Koreans. The missionaries stressed the good news of God's love for all people. It all sounded egalitarian and liberating, even if Christianity in reality and practice was very divided, patriarchal, and hierarchical.

THE POWER OF THE WHITE WESTERN MISSIONARY

Missionaries held a lot of power. Just the mere fact of being white signified power. They had authority and used it to convince Koreans to go to church and convert to Christianity. The American lifestyle, with its convenient appliances and agricultural implements that made life easier, the things they wore, ate, and enjoyed drew a lot of curiosity and envy from Koreans. It was aspirational and inspirational for them.

There were other westerners in Korea at the time, including diplomatic and consular representatives as well as military men, who also demonstrated their superiority through their worldly possessions and use of advanced industrial technology. They reinforced how inferior Koreans were to westerners in cultural, economic, and religious aspects. Missionaries preached the good news that a world far better would follow this world and that the United States was a land of "milk and honey." Koreans began to gain a taste and desire for Western "civilization" and some of its comforts and conveniences. This desire spread across the country[12] as Koreans began to share Christianity with friends and family. White missionaries presented a religion associated with Western science and technology, which at that time was more advanced than Eastern science and technology. It was also presented as a way to gain wealth and a middle-class lifestyle that many poor Koreans desired.

White missionaries' teachings and beliefs made a deep impression on Korea's culture, religion, and economy. They taught that whiteness was good, almost like a gift from God. Koreans were set on a path to emulate white American missionaries. Even after leaving Korea, missionaries' teachings were imprinted on the country and can still be observed today.

Whiteness is still uplifted in many aspects of Korean society. For example, many Korean women still accept the westernization of beauty. They believe their Asian features are not appealing and thus seek to be like white women with larger eyes, double eyelids, narrower and higher noses, fuller lips, and smaller jaw lines. Korean women spend a lot of time and money to whiten their skin through makeup, lotions, and chemicals. They also seek costly plastic surgery procedures to achieve Western standards of female beauty and surgically change their faces to look more like white women.[13] If a Korean wants to become a model in a Western magazine or on a runway, she must alter her appearance to mimic Western beauty. Koreans also adopted Western styles of clothing, dancing, and using knives and forks with some foods, which was never part of Korean eating. These are just some of the influences that whiteness impressed on Korea.

White Christians taught Koreans that they should embrace Western philosophy, culture, and forms of education. The perception of the West being better than the East is indoctrinated into Koreans in all aspects of life. Today, as Korean missionaries go out to other parts of the world to share the good news, it is often the same good news of whiteness that the white missionaries first taught them.

THE WHITE GOOD NEWS

As white Christianity spread, it impacted and molded the identities of people of color around the globe[14] in an attempt to Anglicize these other cultures. Part of the "good news" that was shared was intended to separate people of color from their own cultural heritages and customs and adopt a white Christian identity, practice, and religion.

White Christianity, which was disseminated by European missionaries and adopted through white enslavers, is not the true Christianity that it has routinely positioned itself to be. True Christianity cannot and should not endorse racism, xenophobia, subjugation, discrimination, domination, colonialism, or enslavement. Christianity through the lens of the powerful, the mighty, or the colonialist cannot be the real Christianity of love, liberation, and hope that Jesus shared as he walked the earth. This is not good news. Therefore, it is necessary to recognize the colonizer aspect of white Christianity, unpack and dismiss its defining components, and move toward a Christianity that is truly liberating and empowering for all people of color.[15] If this colonialist white Christianity is not recognized and dismantled, we will fail to see how white supremacy is embedded in white Christianity and how it continues to reinforce whiteness. This is dangerous, unhealthy, and can be deadly.

Christianity was not originally a white European religion. Under the Roman Empire, it became white and spread to different parts of the world through imperialism, colonialism, and evangelism. As a result, Asians gained an inferiority complex around themselves and their heritage. Whiteness is so ingrained in Asian thinking and understanding of Christianity that it continues to hold superiority over their own long history, heritage, and cultural understandings. Asians prefer Western and white scientific research over their own kind. Koreans have embraced white Christianity without trying to contextualize Christianity or make sense of Christianity in Korean culture and society. They embraced a white Jesus who still hangs on the cross and is drawn in the stained-glass windows. They worship a white God who reinforces that whiteness is better than Asianness, and thus embrace white American or white European Christianity.

Those converting to Christianity did not really question the good news of a white Eurocentric Christianity and a white male God but rather embraced it wholeheartedly as the one true gospel. Koreans assumed because the good news came from white people that it must be a white religion, centered on a white God. They embraced a white God, coming to believe that white was good or better than what Koreans had to offer. Koreans have become blind to the veil of whiteness that continues to teach that whiteness is progress, advancement, superiority, and betterment. It was the white missionaries who built up Korea economically after Japanese colonialism and the Korean War. White missionaries helped build some of the best hospitals and universities in Korea, and therefore social and economic progress was intimately tied to white missionaries and white Christianity. Therefore, white Christianity was easily accepted as the key and power to social and economic advancement.

I never realized that white European missionaries were creating and sharing a Jesus made in their own image until I was out of seminary and teaching. The whiteness of Western society prevented me from exploring the evils and problems of a white Christianity. I was taught that Christianity was white and that was the truth. Whiteness is powerful as it prevents us from thinking outside of Western ideology, power, and teachings. The good news from white missionaries was tainted by whiteness.

Discussing the damage to Asians in the name of a white God is important in encouraging people around the world to develop a Christianity that makes sense to them in their own particular contexts and situations. White Christianity does not address their concerns; it maintains subordination of people of color and keeps the status quo. Koreans were hearing the Christian gospel for the first time, so they didn't really challenge what they heard and passively accepted what was presented to them as the truth. Since white Protestant missionaries lived a good life with Western goods and services, it was enticing for many poor Koreans who wanted a piece of it. As a result, Koreans embraced white Christianity as the truth and never questioned or challenged it. This subordination of Koreans and Asians can best be explained through the term *Orientalism*.

Postcolonial theorist Edward Said used the term *Orientalism* to help us understand how the relationship between the East and the West has played out through the eyes of the powerful West. Said believed that Orientalism, or the study of the Orient, was a political vision of reality. The West used Orientalism to promote a binary opposition between the West and the Orient, the East. Europeans invented the Orient to serve their own agenda. Since ancient times, the Orient has been a place of romance and exoticized to show that it was a strange and unusual place.[16] It became a way to promote an "us" versus "them" reality to show the superiority of the West over East. This in turn led to the development of racism, xenophobia, and prejudices against those whose origins were not in the West and hence reinforced whiteness and white supremacy. The result is a stereotypical representation of Asia embodying a colonialist attitude.

Said wrote that Orientalism "is a term to describe the western approach to the Orient. Orientalism is the discipline by which the Orient was (and is) approached systematically, as a topic of learning, discovery, and practice."[17] Said argued that Western powers and people othered the Orient, resulting in negative consequences to Asians. This inferior portrayal and understanding of the Orient by Europeans caused a separation of Europe and others that contributed to the making of European culture and helped maintain and extend European hegemony over other lands.[18] Having control of one's own story and narrative is powerful, and the loss of it is problematic for many generations to come. To know and tell your own story gives you ownership and influence.

Said believed that this binary opposition of comparing itself with Asia was crucial to Europe's self-conception and self-development. It served to create a positive and strong perception of Europe and a negative view of Asia. Based on this line of thinking, if colonized people are irrational then Europeans must be rational. If those in the East are barbaric, sensual, and lazy, then Europe must be civilization itself. Europeans are able to keep their sexual appetites under control and uphold their dominant work ethic, as opposed to Asia. If the Orient is viewed as static and stagnant, then Europe is developing, progressive, and marching ahead to a great future. In addition, if the Orient is feminine and inferior, then Europe is masculine, dominant, superior, and powerful. Various studies of colonialism have shown this dialectic between self and other to be influential in the way it informs colonial attitudes and distorts perceptions of non-European peoples.[19]

Understanding and examining Orientalism helps us see the work of white Western missionaries in Asia through a clearer perspective. They went there with a belief in their own superiority and power, and wanted to convert the inferior heathens. The result was a white Christianity poured onto impressionable Koreans who became convinced the white way of living and being was the ideal.

WHITE DESIRE

Edward Said's work on Orientalism provides insight into what is happening with Christianity. Western theological work is highly valued and viewed as correct while Eastern Christian theology is understood as inferior, syncretistic, and non-truth. For example, German theologian Jürgen Moltmann's pneumatology, rooted in a white, European male's point of view, is viewed as truer than and superior to any Asian pneumatology based on Chi.

As a public theologian and a scholar, I have published numerous books, yet my work is not valued as highly as a white male scholar's work who may have written only one book. Even in the country of my birth, Koreans value scholarship and theology from white men over their own. They believe that white theology is the truth, and numerous white men's theology books get translated into Korean. As I tried to reach out to Korean scholars to translate my work into Korean, it never transpired and, to date, none of my work has been translated into the Korean language. This preference of white theology over an Asian American woman's theology has been a painful reality to accept. This is the impact of Orientalism, which continues to this day in religious understandings and Christian theology.

Today, in Korea and other parts of Asia, it is more acceptable to learn from white theologians, particularly white male theologians, rather than from their own Asian theologians who are living in the diaspora. This is ingrained in them from the teachings of white missionaries a hundred years ago.

I grew up with this same mentality as an immigrant in Canada. My mother and her siblings and in-laws all insisted on the superiority of Western ideas, products, and ways of being. During our first trip back to Korea in 1982, my mother took some Western makeup, vitamins, and dried foods such as banana chips, nuts, chocolates, and clothes to give to her family and friends. The excitement among all my aunts and uncles to see Western products was astounding. I remember one aunt looking at a lipstick and saying the color didn't match her face, but it didn't matter as she still wanted it and would cherish this Western product.

Whiteness affects religion, Christianity, politics, culture, and even language. The English language was promoted in Korea as a language that would help children and young people move up in the social and economic ladder, and it is still emphasized today; even nursery students are placed in English classes to improve their chances at success later in life, and much effort, time, and money are spent learning English. Children are sometimes sent abroad to study in North America so they can learn English quickly and efficiently as parents hope this will open doors and opportunities when they grow up. These young students end up living with relatives or friends, in homestays, or in private boarding schools.

Christianity maintained its whiteness and was spread throughout the world through the "good" work of white missionaries who went into Asia, Africa, South America, and all parts of the world. But white Christianity has negative implications for people of color, immigrants, and refugees who come from all over the world to the United States. Thus, it is vital that we explore how to preach, teach, and live out a Christianity that is for all people around the globe and not just for whites. The next chapter will examine the ongoing consequences of white Christianity.

5

CHRISTIANITY AND WHITENESS

From the time I immigrated to North America in 1975, white supremacy and whiteness have plagued my life. White supremacy is an enormous mountain that, nearly fifty years later, I still cannot seem to surmount. It is so entrenched in our entire cultural system that it seems impossible to destroy. White supremacy keeps lying to me that to be a Canadian or an American, I must reject all of my Asian heritage, religion, cuisines, and culture as inferior. I have been cautioned that in order to become a good and worthy person I needed to divorce myself from my heritage and take on white culture. As a young child, I was in constant psychological turmoil and distress as I tried to rid myself of my Asianness.

We have been misled by the notion that America's "melting pot" makes us all equal. The truth is that rather than make us equal, this blending is a homogenization into whiteness, prioritizing and idealizing white culture. This was the motivating factor for sending Native Americans and First Nations peoples to Christian boarding schools where they were told lies about how barbaric their own history, culture, and customs are, and they were instructed to turn from their ways and become more like white people. These untruths led to their disenfranchisement, disillusionment, and fragmented lives. Similarly, immigrants of color in the United States were told to reject Asian, Black, and South American heritages and ways of being, as they were inferior to white culture.

During this process of trying to assimilate into whiteness at school, I came to resent my parents, my country of birth, and all Asian heritage that my family had instilled in me. It was an ongoing battle within my body and mind. I was embarrassed by my Korean language and told my parents not to use Korean with me in public. I was angry at them for not being able to converse in proper English like the white parents at school. I wanted to look like the rest of the kids at school so they would not taunt me and make fun of my Asian features. I wanted to look less Asian and more white.

The rupture in my identity tormented me. My parents dragged my older sister and me kicking and screaming to Korean language school. I saw no value in it because I wanted to erase my Korean-ness and become white like the rest of the kids at school. I hated learning about my Korean heritage. I hated eating Korean food when I got home from school and wanted to eat what the white kids were eating at home. I never appreciated the time, effort, and pain involved for my mother to make our traditional foods like large jars of kimchi, which is a full day of washing, cutting, salting, and rewashing cabbage to ferment. I begged my mom to stop wasting time making something that was so embarrassing to non-Koreans at school and in the neighborhood. The smell, appearance, and taste of kimchi was shameful to my whole being.

I never appreciated the long hours of work that went into all of my mother's cooking, which was devoured quickly without any gratitude toward my mom. It is one of the deepest regrets I carry. To this day I wish I could ask for her forgiveness for my lack of appreciation for her and our culture.

I didn't appreciate the rich religious, political, and cultural history of Korea. Due to being infected by whiteness, everything

Korean was like an allergic reaction to me. When I was young, I just wanted to shed everything Korean about me. I just wanted to become like the white cool kids at school who ate foods that didn't smell of ginger and garlic and to speak eloquent English like a native. All of these things came about as a result of the problem of whiteness, which teaches us that white is best and that people of color are not good, or at least not as good.

IMMIGRATION TO NORTH AMERICA

For as long as white settlers have been in North America, there have also been migrants coming from around the globe including South America, Central America, Asia, and Australia. Asians worked as indentured slaves and faced discrimination. They worked for lower wages on the railway performing the most dangerous tasks, such as blowing up mountains. Many had incurred huge debts getting to North America and had difficulty paying it back. After the Chinese Exclusion Act of 1882, Chinese immigrants were required to carry documentation papers with them at all times and were prevented from voting and holding property. They couldn't testify in court, and it was very difficult to leave the country to visit their home and family. Japanese Americans lost all of their possessions and were sent to internment camps during WWII. They lived in harsh conditions in rooms that were hot in the summer and very cold in the winter. Not only did they lose physical possessions, they also lost their dignity, health, and humanity living in those terrible camps.

Additionally, hate crimes committed against Asians and Asian Americans are nothing new. One of the largest lynchings in America history happened in Los Angeles's Chinatown in 1871 where nineteen Chinese were lynched and murdered. People often associate lynching with African Americans, but it happened to other groups of people as well. And again, we saw a surge of hate crimes during the Covid-19 pandemic where elderly and young Asian women were beaten, kicked, yelled at, and even murdered. The Atlanta spa shooting in 2021 resulted in the murder of eight people in a rampage at three spas. Six out of the eight murdered were Asian, and this violent act has become an ongoing pattern.

To address these hate crimes, it is necessary to understand history, culture, and law. These crimes against the Asian American community arise from exclusionary immigration policy, mob violence, and segregation as well as sexual objectification of Asian American women.[1] There were many unprovoked attacks against Asian Americans who were just walking on the streets, waiting for a subway, going home after work, and other mundane activities. These were targeted acts of hate against Asian Americans, especially the vulnerable such as elderly and women.

Oppression, xenophobia, and discrimination against immigrants of color were present from the beginning and have continued in the form of racialization. As immigrant Christians find their voices, they often expose the problem of racism in the United States and Canada, which is evident also in the life of the churches. A white Christianity, a white God, and a white Jesus are promoted to immigrants of color as the ideal, the goal being to subordinate their status within church and society.

THE IDEALIZATION OF RACIAL IDENTITY

Racialization is a process within the social construction of race that forms race as different and unequal as it pertains to economic, political, and social life. The concepts of race, racialization, racism, and white privilege become embedded into the very fabric of society that determine the system of race relations in the United States and Canada.[2] This race system's mission is to keep people in their place and maintain the status quo. The powerful keep their status and the powerless remain subordinate and subjugated.

When I was in Korea, my family didn't view me as yellow. Asians don't view themselves as yellow, just as Africans do not view themselves as Black. It is only when Africans come to the United States that they come to see themselves as Black. This is the racialization process, which labels us according to our skin color. Along with the division of people according to skin color is the understanding of a hierarchy of color, with white being at the top.

People of color approach racial identity differently than those who identify as white. People of color must consider their racial identity in every situation and context where they find themselves. This happens due to the systemic and interpersonal racism that exists in all spheres of society.[3] During the peak of the Covid-19 pandemic, the AAPI community's awareness of racial identity was even more heightened, and we all carried a keen awareness that we could fall victim to a hate crime even as we walked to work, returned home, and rode buses and subways. We were aware that we could not escape racialization, and we must remain on alert for any potential vocal or physical attacks. This is what it means to have to be conscious of racial identity daily. We live in fear that we, or a close relative, might be the next victim of racialized hate crimes.

This is not something white people need to be conscious of, while people of color carry this fear constantly. When we say white people exist in privilege, power, and substance, it isn't just related to material things. It includes their very existence—the degree of safety and security they enjoy on a daily basis. They have created a society where they are powerful, and the structure of that society ensures they retain their power.

But people of color do not exist to prop up white people or whiteness. Systemic racism blames people of color if anything goes wrong in our society. It diminishes the way we are valued in society when we are constantly the scapegoats for societal ills that are often the responsibility of white people.

White people tend to gloss over microaggressions and institutional problems that are fundamentally racist. However, racism must be named and categorized in order for society to view and understand. The atrocities committed against people of color will continue to occur if we do not eradicate racism. The cycle of vicious racism needs to be broken.

WHITENESS

Racism destroys and kills. It creates turmoil and suffering. As long as laws, rules, workplace behaviors, and societal structures do not change, racism will continue. The way we view and understand God, Jesus, humanity, and the church is intrinsic to the shift away from systemic racism. New liberative ways of believing and perceiving God need to be reconstructed and reimagined so that we can work toward eliminating racism from our churches, neighborhoods, workplaces, and society.

White-dominant society seeks to insulate white people from addressing their own racial biases so they are never made to feel uncomfortable. Whiteness or the white washing of our daily lives obscures the truth and reality about racism. Whiteness fails to recognize the racialization of white people. White people do not acknowledge how they are also racialized. Since white people view themselves as the standard of humanity, they do not see themselves as the problem. They do not recognize the false elevation of their status or the harm caused to others in this process.

Racism, discrimination, and xenophobia are not just racial slurs hurled on people of color or cross burnings and lynching. Racism arises out of this construct of whiteness, which indoctrinates all people to believe that white people are—naturally and through God's ordinances—just better people. Racism becomes institutionalized as whiteness is perceived as fact rather than a social construct.

Shortly after I moved from Canada to the United States in 2004 to teach, we took a family trip to a Sears department store to buy a new dryer for our apartment. My children were only five, three, and one years old at that time. As we roamed around looking for the most affordable dryer, two Sears employees walked toward us. I was glad to see them as I needed help in deciding which dryer to purchase. They saw my little girl first and one of them lowered his body and said "ching chong, ching chong" to my little girl. *Ching chong* is a racial pejorative term used to mock Asians. It is a term that often accompanied assaults and physical intimidation of Asians. I was devastated to see this happening right before my eyes with my three-year-old daughter. I quickly grabbed her and left the store. Later that day, I called the manager to complain. They explained that the employee had just returned from eating Chinese food for lunch. I do not understand why they thought that was any justification for their racist behavior. After a long conversation, I realized this manager and his employees would not comprehend the level of pain that they caused my family. Racism is excused and ignored as something trivial. But the wounds go deep for those who experience racism.

Racism appears in various forms within our society. It is sometimes so embedded in our society that we fail to detect its presence; in addition, it permeates even the most liberal institutions, and white progressives who believe they aren't and can't be racist are still influenced by whiteness. These fallacies blind whites to the racist roots they carry and how deeply those roots go in society.

This leads to the tokenization of people of color and results in their being further discriminated against and marginalized.

Describing racism and discrimination as ignorant feelings of superiority based on skin color enables white people to exonerate themselves of racism even though this problem is systemic and embedded in society and culture. When white people believe they are not racist, they express indignation and resentment when accused of racism or racists acts. They believe they cannot be racist because they voted for a Black president and have friends and coworkers who are people of color. Racism is not just an overt belief of white superiority but also a complicity to an ideology that there is a racial hierarchy. One cannot just be nice to people and communities of color. White people must act and change their structures and the power dynamics that allow racism to occur.

Dismantling racism is an enormous task, but it must be done if we want a society for all people and not just for white people. Being confronted with the problems of whiteness challenges the notion of white being better because of intrinsic goodness, and that creates a cognitive dissonance that white people can't handle. It is easier to simply move on to other topics or just "try to get along" instead of examining now they are complicit in allowing racist social structures to continue. People of color can't just get along with white people or just move on, as this will not eliminate racism and racist behaviors.[4] Pretending it doesn't exist does not stop innocent young Black men from being shot and killed by police, Asian American women from being targeted and murdered, Latinx people from being stereotyped and discriminated against, and Native American communities from being disenfranchised.

In my first teaching job there came a time when problems started to arise among some of the students. During a faculty and staff meeting about the issue, a white staff blurted out, "We decided to hire people of color, and look at all the problems that they bring." People of color are continually assigned blame when things go wrong in society, churches, and workplaces. White people find it difficult to see where they are contributing to the problem or may, in fact, be the problem.

Oppression occurs in various forms and is intertwined and intersectional. Intersectionality reminds us that our identities are complex and not just one-dimensional. We all have multiple layers to our identities. For example, I am a Korean, straight, able-bodied, educated, immigrant woman. Recognizing the intersectionality of oppression enables us to understand how oppression works. Intersectionality pushes us forward to try and overturn these various aspects of oppression, which continue to marginalize and subjugate us. Recognizing the multifaceted aspects of oppression ignites us to work together to fight white supremacy. We must work together to obtain gender justice, economic justice, climate justice, and eradicate all other injustices that oppress and subordinate groups of people. White people need to relinquish their power, entitlement, belongingness, economy, and riches so that communities of color will have a fighting chance. If this does not happen, then problems will continue to perpetuate.

WHITE SUPREMACY AND CHRISTIANITY

The rise and spread of white Christianity in Europe led to many forms of white supremacy within Christianity. Christianity today is overwhelmingly white Eurocentric in Western/American Christian contexts, including its practices and doctrines, which is inevitably detrimental to people of color. Churches and other institutions are guilty of upholding white supremacy and allowing it to be institutionalized by establishing whiteness as the shining model of Christianity.[5] The whiteness in Christianity is what many nonwhite churches are aspiring to. But whiteness limits our humanity, and it conveys to people of color that we are not worthy, that we are not precious in God's sight because we are not white.

One of the ways white supremacy furthers Eurocentrism is redefining terms to whitewash them. Jim Crow laws are now "states' rights." White affirmative action becomes "merit-based selection." In this way, people who share the rhetoric of freedom can justify acts that have brought death, enslavement, and harm to so many people. The sanitization of these terms allows for the imposition of white, patriarchal, and heteronormative standards upon a nation seeking liberation from Eurocentric puritanical beliefs.

Furthermore, religious oppression is carried out in other disguises. Controlling the bodies of women safeguards heterosexual male rights under the banner of "religious freedom." But what white male Christians are really doing is advocating for domination of the other by redefining oppression as an attack on religious freedom.[6] Religion is invoked frequently in an attempt to sanctify behaviors and ideas that are simply white supremacy, patriarchy, and white Christian supremacy. At times, there is no distinction between them, which is why we must become hypervigilant to bring awareness around the true identity of Christianity.

Throughout the history of Christian theology, all the major theologians have portrayed God as male and white. For example, Anselm of Canterbury presents a theory of atonement that portrays God as a European feudal lord. Martin Luther uses male pronouns to speak about God and talks about God as ruler of the two kingdoms. These are masculine attributes and ideals. The problem with this representation is that it stratifies and systematizes a faith that is supposed to embrace the idea that all people are equal. This social understanding has damaged all other ethnic groups and led to the attempted destruction of other cultures.

Miguel De La Torre states that white Christianity embraces and teaches a worldview of manifest destiny of white bodies to occupy the highest echelons of power, profit, and privilege due solely to their light skin hue and nothing else. As a result, people of color are marginalized and must relinquish whatever power that they have. *White* as an adjective to share a distorted version of Christianity fails to signify skin pigmentation nor physiognomy as *white* becomes a neutral term.[7] This embracing of white supremacy asserts the wrong belief that manifest destiny, the Doctrine of Discovery, conquest, colonialism, and empire are the will of God. White supremacy robs white people's ability to be in right relationships with fellow citizens, with themselves, and with God. It is so blended and burrowed in Christianity that it becomes very difficult to divorce white supremacy from Christianity.

Though white Christians may try to achieve reconciliation with people of color, they need to seek justice instead. Reconciliation suggests a restoration of a previously amicable relationship, of making two things realigned. However, that cannot be when there has never been alignment or equity between whites and people of color. To restore that relationship would mean taking things back to the way they were when people of color were silent and obedient. That offers no healing. White supremacy must be eradicated from institutions, religion, and white people's psyches so they can move beyond forgetfulness, amnesia, and silence[8] and into some form of action that will work for change and integrity. White Christians need to put time into living into the full promise of justice and liberty for all.

White Christians need to understand and unpack their whiteness and recognize their white privilege, which has led to harm toward people of color. Making sure they understand themselves is a big step toward working to eliminate racism and building a racially just world. White people can examine their own privilege at work, in their community and in faith communities. Remembering their white privilege and how it gets translated into Christianity and Christian practice is a major step toward healing choices to eliminate whiteness from Christianity. Songs, hymns, prayers, and liturgical choices that reflect a global contextual understanding of faith and Christianity would be a major step toward justice.

While white Christianity is declining in the West, local indigenous Christianity is slowly growing in the Global South, and Christianity is increasingly African, Asian, and Latin American. As Christianity expands in the Global South, we need to be welcoming of the indigenous voices and how Christianity becomes contextualized in other locations around the world. Contextualizing Christianity and trying to make sense of it in different cultures will help it move away from whiteness. The different theological voices that emerge from around the globe should naturally become part of the white-dominant Christianity. These different perspectives and approaches should challenge white Christianity. Christianity has never been pristine and has always been affected by context and local cultures and religions. Therefore even today, Christianity needs to be open, to adapt and to be moved by these emerging Global South perspectives, practices, and leanings. Ultimately, this only enriches, and deepens our Christian faith and practice.

THE MISAPPROPRIATION OF NATIONALISM

Nationalism is the understanding that people can be divided into mutually distinct cultural groups defined by shared language, religion, ethnicity, and culture. Nationalists believe that these groups should each have their own governments, which can protect a nation's cultural identity. Christian nationalism is the understanding that America is defined by Christianity and that the government should take important steps to maintain that identity. They assert that America is and must remain a "Christian nation" and Christianity should have a privileged position in the public square.[9] They paint a picture of America being chosen by God to become a Christian nation, a perspective that distorts Scripture to validate their own wishes and desires.

I have served as pulpit supply minister for many years and have visited a lot of churches where the American flag is lifted higher than the cross. This is not just exclusive to America; I have seen a few Canadian churches do the same thing. This only serves to reinforce for some white Christians that Christianity and nationalism are interwoven.

Allowing white culture to become more important than faith has led to the emergence of a prideful and nationalistic Christianity rather than a Christianity focused on the oppressed and the marginalized, as Christians are called to do. Christian nationalism is strong in America and denies people of color their individual agency while also ignoring the importance of their contributions to the church. We must be reminded that Christianity does not belong to America or to England or to France. Christianity does not belong to any one country; on the contrary, the Bible instructs us to go into all the world and share the gospel. Historians understand that neither Jesus nor his disciples were white but were deeply olive-skinned Semites. They did not speak English, as many readers of the King James Version and red-letter Bibles want to believe. And there is a fervent commodification of Christianity as countless churches and megachurches are erected and frequently bear toxic leadership and corrupt clergy who influence the moral beliefs of people.[10] Church members follow what the leaders preach, teach, and model for them. Capitalism within the church is a dangerous cycle for Christianity.

White Christian nationalism reinforces white supremacy and a white male patriarchal Christianity by normalizing oppressive policies and laws imposed on people of color and carrying on with the dishonest narratives of the supposed dangers and problems they represent to white America. Linking the phrase *religious liberty* to fears and misconceptions about what religion is supposed to look like normalizes and legitimizes the othering of people of color. When something goes wrong in church or society, or when conventions change, white Christian nationalists quickly accuse people of color. When the economy fails, people of color are at fault. When white students are passed over for admissions to top colleges and universities, foreigners are blamed. Christian nationalism wants to maintain the status quo without any form of disruption or challenge. Christian nationalism does not want to remember the genocide against Native Americans, enslavement of Africans, indenturing of Asian workers, or taking of land from Mexico.[11] They want to recollect their whitewashed version of history where they were the white savior to Native Americans and people of color. They create their own history of good mission work and rescuing heathens from their innate savagery. This way of thinking and remembrance is not Christian, and it should not be linked to Christianity any longer. It should just be called as it truly is, white nationalism.

Christian nationalism creates great division and discord both in society and in the church. America cannot move forward if Christian nationalism is in place, as an insurrection like January 6, 2021, will happen again and again. Christianity should not be viewed solely through the eyes of white male European Christians, but through the lens of all Christians, which includes women and people of color. These different lenses will help work toward correcting the wronged beliefs about what Christianity really is.

Christian nationalism distorts the good news to serve whiteness[12] and white people. We need to work toward eliminating a white gospel before it does further damage. Rejecting Christian nationalism should not be confused with rejection of Christianity as they are not the same thing. We need to remove the Eurocentric lenses by which Christianity is seen, defined, and preached. We need to be aware of the other lenses through which we can come to see Christianity and live out Christianity that is so different from Eurocentric practices and teachings. The more lenses that we use to live out our Christianity, the better and deeper our understanding of God will be. God is infinite and we humans are finite beings with limitations, flaws, and inconsistencies. The more languages, words, and lenses that we adopt and utilize, the deeper and richer our understanding of God will be.

Christianity should help us see through the lens of the disenfranchised, the marginalized, and the oppressed, just as Jesus did during his ministry. Jesus shared the gospel of liberation and good news for the poor. Christianity has long forgotten this message as it seeks to build empires, to colonize, and to enslave. While nationalism can serve to preserve a national identity, it has no place in Christianity. We must reclaim the real good news of liberty, freedom, equality, and love.

One way for churches to begin to see through a different lens is celebrate events that focuses on different people such as Asian American Heritage Month, Native American Indian Heritage Month, and National Immigrant Heritage Month to remember and welcome new people into the faith community. These events can be moments of education, celebration, and remembering of the many different contributions that people from various backgrounds and heritages make to society and to Christianity. These celebrations and educational events will deepen the church community's commitment to diversity, growth, and observance of differences. It is so important to welcome, embrace, and love the various cultures, histories, and traditions of different peoples around the globe as it helps us love those who are so different from us. Learning different faith songs, hymns, and practices will enrich the traditional white congregation's life and ministry.

DISMANTLING WHITE SUPREMACY AND WHITENESS

Dismantling racism and building coalitions between people of color requires widening the discourse on racism to include all people of color. We cannot limit the conversation to black and white. We must engage in a larger discourse that includes Native Americans, Hispanics and Latinx, and Asian Americans. Otherwise racism will continue to curtail and dominate the American narrative.[13]

This book began by looking at whiteness and how whiteness is the basis for racism, xenophobia, discrimination, and a long list of atrocities committed in North America and around the world. If this devastating problem is not challenged and rooted out, we will continue to have these problems not only in society but also in the church. It will continue to poison the American soul.

There are ramifications to a white Christianity, and its impact is felt in politics, culture, society, and religion. The impact is not only a white faith, but a "gospel" of how whites are superior to other races and how white Western ways of living are the standard that everyone else should try to achieve in their own societies and communities. This whiteness of the gospel is based on a white Jesus who never existed.

We cannot work toward eliminating racism from our society until we unpack and understand whiteness and its true impact. Naming whiteness doesn't mean we don't like white people, just as calling out sexism doesn't mean that we hate all men. We simply need to recognize whiteness as a system that takes up space and rarely allows people of color to move forward or move up. It consumes too much air in Christianity, politics, culture, philosophy, and history. And white people spend too much time justifying, dismissing, or denying the problem and not enough time listening.

The experience and expertise of people of color must be recognized and respected. We cannot allow white people to define us and our spaces. We also cannot allow whiteness to define God and Christianity. Immigrants make North America a diverse, rich, beautiful, and changing society. And Christian immigrants are challenging and changing worship, faith practices, and understandings of white Eurocentric Christianity. Immigrants from other faith traditions are also changing Christianity and Christian practices as the clash and colliding of religions encourage people to engage in interfaith dialogue. This is a necessary tool that can dissipate the fear of other faith traditions. We need to engage with one another and learn from one another, especially those who are so different from us. This will deepen our own Christian faith and build new Christian traditions going forward.

6

A WHITE JESUS

How did we start worshiping a white, male God? I know that in my own life, I was never allowed to question or challenge the idea of a white, male God. It was considered sinful to question anything taught by the church or written in the Bible. At church, I was taught to just listen, believe, and obey whatever was taught by ministers and Sunday school teachers. Questioning what was said was not what good Christians did. So I lived my faith without having any doubts until I went to seminary.

Through my seminary studies, I learned to challenge everything about God and Christianity. The endless questions led me to a PhD in theology to explore all things God. But after a rigorous PhD program, I was left with even more questions than answers. One of the biggest questions I sought to answer was, Who is Jesus?

When I was growing up, our days in elementary school began with recitation of the Lord's Prayer, singing of the national anthem, and school announcements. In a multicultural and multireligious society, reciting the Lord's Prayer in a public school was a strong indication of Christian nationalism at play. As a young immigrant girl, I had no idea what I was reciting and memorizing, but I did it religiously every morning just like the white kids in class. It was clear to me that this was something I had to do to be accepted and fit in.

It really wasn't a message of hope and good news instilled in me when I was a young girl; rather it was a message of whiteness from my white elementary school and a white-dominant society. We were bombarded with constant and daily impositions of whiteness. The message was clear: to be a good immigrant of color, conformity with the national white norm was imperative. Conversion to Christianity was the only way to be accepted into this white-dominant society. Of course, this did not apply to white European immigrants—even those who did not speak English—because the color of the skin is what matters most.

We lived in an enclave with many Korean immigrant families. There were three identical apartment buildings, and the middle apartment building where my family lived had the largest number of Korean immigrant families. Out of sixty apartment units, six units were occupied by Korean families, many of whom attended the Korean Presbyterian church, which became a social center for immigrant families. Many non-Christian Koreans who experienced feelings of loneliness and isolation went to church as the Korean church provided a place for connection and community. Finding non-Korean friends and joining white social circles was difficult because of the language barrier. But the bigger barrier was racism in this white-dominant society. One of the common attacks on us came from the fact that our apartments had to be fumigated regularly due to the cockroach infestations. It was a horrible mess to clean up each time—cleaning all surfaces of the chemical residue and the dead bugs that resulted. The superintendent would tell others, "We have bugs because the Asians brought them." The bugs were there before any of us came, but we bore the blame because we were outsiders.

Most of the Korean immigrants worked multiple jobs, which meant they did not have opportunities to engage with coworkers and socialize after work. This complicated their integration into society. This was post-Korean War when the economy was weak and immigration to North America was on the rise. In America, we use the term *people of color* to refer to nonwhites. In Canada, we used the term *visible minority*. If a white European individual immigrates, their whiteness allows them to integrate more easily than those who are nonwhite. Nonwhites are visibly different, which makes us more easily othered.

One of the oddest jobs my parents had when I was young was picking earthworms. There is a big market for them particularly with gardeners and people who fish. My parents went out late at night to several different golf courses to pick the worms. Golf courses did not want worms on their courses, so picking worms was a service for them. My parents were too embarrassed to tell my sister and me what they were doing in the middle of the night. But one day, I overheard my dad sharing with his friends how difficult this job was. They went with a cheap headlamp strapped to their heads and tin cans which hung from their waist to pick up earthworms all night long on the golf course. My mom was not particularly good with animals or natural things so she first wore gloves as a form of protection. But the worms would slip from her gloves, so she had to adjust to using her bare hands. She described how slimy and slippery these worms were, how they crouched low, careful not to shine the light where it would scare the worms away, and they did this all night. It was back-breaking, filthy work. They were paid by the pound, and it didn't add up to much. My parents didn't have many options for earning money. Picking earthworms was a job that no one wanted, but immigrants did it to survive. It was seen as degrading work, but it put food on the table.

96

WHEN GOD BECAME WHITE

Since Asian culture is centered around the honor/shame dichotomy, I never shared with anyone—friends, strangers, or relatives—what my parents did for a living. I knew my mother was ashamed that she went from a housewife in Korea to picking earthworms in the middle of the night to just make a living. I have never shared this with anyone until the writing of this book. The shame that my mother carried was also a shame that I carried alongside her. I could not believe that a kind, beautiful loving mother had to resort to picking dirty, slimy earthworms to put food on the table; it was both degrading and painful for me to witness. Even though my mother did that in the evenings, in the daytime while working in a garment factory, she never let anyone know about her night job.

THE IMMIGRANT CHURCH AND FAITH LIFE

The Korean immigrants in this era lived isolated and lonely lives. For many, attending church was a source of deep comfort, solace, and peace. The church became an extended family, and birthday parties, weddings, anniversaries, and other celebrations were an important part of that, sharing meals, presents, and laughter together. Connecting with other Koreans through church became the way of finding community and life. Since we didn't have any extended family in Canada, every celebration was done in conjunction with church and church friends. The church quickly became family to us.

At the beginning, it was only my sister and I who attended the Korean Presbyterian church. Mrs. Kim (no relation to us), who lived on the third floor of our apartment building, urged us to attend church. She drove us every Sunday to church and then brought us back home safely. After a year, my parents decided to join us at church to make connections. My dad is the social butterfly in the family and loves to meet people and socialize. My mother was the quiet, homebody type. My dad felt the social need to attend the church to get connected to more Korean immigrants. Though my mother didn't feel the same need, my dad was the head of the house, so my mother followed and obeyed.

Once my parents started attending church, everything became strict in the home, and we lived very conservative, Christian lives. We were allowed to listen to only Christian music and gospel songs. We were not allowed to shop on Sundays, and we were not allowed to go to school dances because they were considered the work of the devil. My dad literally told me that dancing, or jumping up and down in a club, is exactly what people do in hell due to the heat. He said that those who dance are rehearsing what they will be doing in hell. My dad would scare me by telling me awful stories about hell all the time. I am sure he did some psychological damage to me as a child as I would act out of fear around him for the fear of going to hell after death.

Additionally, we were not to smoke or drink, these being essentially the eleventh and twelfth Commandments. My mother made my sister and me fast on Good Friday. It was a yearly ritual that started when we were only eight and nine years old. My mother however, fasted for three days—from Good Friday to Easter. I had a hard time fasting as a young girl. One year I found some coins lying around in the living room, so I put them in my pocket and without thinking I made the fifteen-minute walk to the neighborhood corner store around 10:30 in the morning. In the 1980s, stores had penny candies that were popular among young children. At the store, I bought as many penny candies as I could. The loose change I'd discovered added up to a tiny brown paper bag full of candies, small enough to fit in the palm of my hand. But that was enough candy to satisfy a fasting girl. I started to eat them immediately, but halfway through the bag, I felt an enormous uneasiness in my stomach. I could hear my mother yelling about the disgrace of not fasting on Good Friday. I felt so guilty I couldn't eat the rest of the candies.

A WHITE JESUS AT HOME

Our family and social lives centered on the Korean church. But that wasn't enough. We were also taken to a white Baptist church and a Missionary Alliance church for Bible studies, fellowship, and worship. On Sunday mornings, they dropped us off at one Baptist church for Sunday school. Then, on Sunday evenings, we went to yet another very small Baptist church for Sunday night worship. All of these churches offered exciting Christian worship, study, and fun. However, in every church I attended, a white Jesus with fair skin, blue eyes and blond hair was worshiped and presented to me. The Sunday school teachers used curricula with pictures of a white Jesus. We sang hymns and children's songs that were very white and learned a lot about a white, male God. We sang songs like "Father Abraham Had Many Sons," and the church showed pictures of a white Abraham and white Sarah. I didn't even know that the Old Testament was a sacred Jewish text until much later in my youth. I just thought everything I was taught at church from the Old Testament and New Testament was written by white Europeans.

The white, male Jesus I learned about at church and saw in the painting my mother hung in a prominent place in our childhood apartment was engrained in my body and my mind. It was instilled into my faith system that repeatedly affirmed the goodness of being white people. God is white, Jesus is white and, therefore, white people are the closest to God. This white Christianity was part of my faith until my adulthood, and it took me a long time to unpack, dismantle, and reimagine God as nonwhite. The path was not an easy one to endeavor.

Jesus has been portrayed as white for generations, and we need to ask how Jesus *became* white and what its implications are for church and society. We also need to understand why Christians ended up worshiping a white, male God, which affects all aspects of society whether one is religious or not.

WHITE JESUS INVENTED

No one knows what Jesus looked like. Unlike today where people document everything they do, from eating to walking to working, with pictures on their cell phone, there are no images of Jesus from his lifetime over two thousand years ago. But we can reasonably deduce that he was dark, with dark eyes and olive skin. He was born in the Middle East and his family fled to Egypt where they lived for a part of his life. Had he been light skinned, his family would not have been able to blend with the Egyptians and they would have been in danger.

Joan Taylor, a professor of Christian origins and Second Temple Judaism, researched what Jesus could have looked like. She studied holy artifacts such as the Veronica cloth or the Turin Shroud to look for clues about how Jesus looked. She also studied archaeological artifacts such as coins, textiles and well-preserved human remains from Jesus' time to find further clues. Her findings suggest that Jesus was around five feet, five inches tall, with brown eyes, black hair, olive-brown skin, and probably wore a simple one-piece tunic.[1] This image is so different from our present-day white European Jesus that we have come to welcome and worship. Furthermore, Isaiah 53:2 states, "He had no form or majesty that we should look at him, nothing in his appearance that we should desire him." Thus Jesus was not attractive or handsome as Christians have continuously portrayed him to be.

So how did an olive-brown-skinned Jesus become white, and what is the purpose of having a white Jesus and a white God? It has to do with power. A white Jesus and a white God are created and reinforced by the desires of those who held power and authority. During the Roman Empire, an olive-brown-skinned Jesus was not useful for the expansion of their empire and kingdom. They needed a white Jesus who resembled them to validate their dominance, dominion, and authority. An olive-skinned Jewish Jesus would have opened the door to there being a different authority, so he became white with blue eyes and blond hair to resemble those who were already in power—the Roman Empire. This transformation was quickly accepted and embraced by white European Christian men who were making Jesus and God in their own image. Jesus was changed into an emperor of high stature, good looks and beautiful clothes.

White male Eurocentric Christianity, which emerged during the Greco-Roman period, was maintained and sustained during the spread of Christianity throughout Europe. Jesus was conveyed as a white, male European Lord, and God was understood to be an old, white man sitting on a throne high up in the sky. The European-looking Jesus can be traced back to the Byzantine period (330 CE) when artists wanted to represent the "son of God." They were probably inspired by already existing godly figures like Zeus and Apollo. This explains the similarity of Jesus' depictions to Zeus's long hair and beard, and Apollo-like slim and delicate features. It is also at this time that he is shown wearing a royal robe, as opposed to the one-piece tunic he most likely wore.[2] Images of Jesus were given an elevated look to make him kingly and godly like their own European kings and gods.

There was a lot of messaging and branding that went into how Jesus was depicted. For example, in a mosaic from Santa Puden-ziana, the oldest surviving Catholic church in Rome, built be-tween 384 and 398, Jesus was portrayed as "pantocrator" and as a ruler-judge at the end of the world. Jesus is presented to the world as an imperial leader wearing a lavish gold garment, which was classic Zeus and Jupiter clothing and not what Jesus most likely wore. His posture is also painted like imperial emperor Au-gustus, holding out his right arm to the viewer's left as a gesture of law-maintaining authority. His long, baggy sleeves were in-spired by the *dalmatica* worn by the upper classes in the Byzantine era. After this Byzantine period the imperial ruler image of Jesus was cemented and spread around the world through colonialism and missionaries.[3] Jesus became molded into the images of the European leaders and their gods. This helped legitimize their power over their own people as well as others around the world through colonialism and domination.

During the European Renaissance (1350–1600 CE), Leonardo da Vinci's *Last Supper* and Michelangelo's *Last Judgment* were painted on the ceiling in the Sistine Chapel. Both of these depic-tions of Jesus as white, European, and upper-class have deeply influenced our present-day image and belief of who Jesus is. The most widely reproduced image is Warner Sallman's light-eyed, light-haired image of Jesus called the *Head of Christ,* painted in 1940. This picture was widely marketed worldwide through two Christian publishing companies. Sallman's painting culminates the long tradition of white Europeans inventing a white Jesus.[4] It was so widely believed that this was the "true" image and likeness of Jesus, that Brown, Black, and Asian people around the globe hung this image in their churches, homes, and offices as a way to exhibit their Christian faith and belief in Jesus.

This prominent white Jesus is so ingrained in our psyche that it is sometimes very difficult to erase it from our minds. Korean Presbyterian churches like the one I grew up in are very conservative and taught us not to question their teachings. Paired with the Confucian culture of my heritage, which requires obedience from women, I was fully indoctrinated into blind acceptance of what my elders and leaders told me was true. But, as I got older and saw the difficulties arising from my understanding of Jesus as a white male, I came to see that it needed to be dismantled to get to the heart of the Christian message. Representation matters as images impact and deeply forms our thoughts, ideas, and understandings. A white image of Jesus informed us that God must also be white.

WHITE JESUS AND THE BIBLE

The white European early churches found it easy to make Jesus white as there are biblical references to white being good, pure, and beautiful and Black being associated with night and evil. The equating of whiteness with purity and goodness in the Bible created the perfect vehicle for whitewashing Jesus. The notion of the color white as good has been transferred to Jesus, who is seen as pure, perfect and holy. John 1:29 states, "Here is the Lamb of God who takes away the sin of the world." Lambs are depicted as white and pure even though they come in different colors. Think of the nursery rhyme: "Mary had a little lamb; its fleece was white as snow." This imagery of Jesus as the pure sacrificial Lamb of God reinforces and sustains the idea of Jesus being white.

Scripture also states, "If your sins are like scarlet, will they become like snow? If they are red like crimson, will they become like wool?" (Isaiah 1:18). Sin is bad and we are stained/tainted by it, but once we are forgiven, we will be made white as snow. The perpetual focus on white imagery in the Bible as an indicator of goodness and purity alienates people of color.

In the creation story in Genesis, God created light:

> When God began to create the heavens and the earth, the earth was complete chaos, and darkness covered the face of the deep, while a wind from God swept over the face of the waters. Then God said, "Let there be light," and there was light. And God saw that the light was good, and God separated the light from the darkness. (Genesis 1:1-4)

The constant dichotomy between light and darkness further emphasizes that God and Jesus must be light rather than dark.

The biblical imagery also connects the Holy Spirit to whiteness. The Spirit, a member of the Trinity, is depicted as a white dove. When Jesus was baptized, "just as he came up from the water, suddenly the heavens were opened to him and he saw God's Spirit descending like a dove and alighting on him" (Matthew 3:16). The biblical reinforcement of white being pure, clean, and righteous is found in other parts of Scripture as well and helped solidify the whiteness of Jesus. In a dualistic world, white is good and black is evil, so there can't possibly be a black Jesus. The biblical images of white and dark helped create a white Jesus. In the nineteenth century, Jesus was made even whiter with the rise of antisemitism. People forget Jesus was a Middle Eastern Jew.[5] With this distinction created between black and white, Jesus can be made even whiter. This argument completely ignores the reality of Jesus' ethnicity. We must ask why the lie of a white Jesus has been perpetuated and search for the original dark-skinned Jesus who preached a gospel of liberation for the poor, the marginalized, the outcast, and the powerless. It is important to begin exploring the fallacy of a white Jesus and how that affects the perception, identification, and understanding of people of color.

DUALISM PAVING THE WAY FOR A WHITE JESUS

In John 8:12, Jesus says, "I am the light of the world," which means he is pure and good. Jesus came into the world to bring light into darkness. Jesus is the light, and light is goodness and stands in contrast to the darkness, which is evil and bad. The writer of John lived in a dualistic world, and he incorporates that dualism into the imagery of Jesus as the light in a dark and evil world. Darkness and light are separate and cannot be brought together.

Dualism is very problematic as it divides the world into two categories in which there can be no harmony. In this dualistic world, Jesus can only be viewed as white and male as both categories are lauded as good and desirable. The feminine is on the opposite end of the spectrum from the male.

Within dualism, we also see the contrast of knowledge, or the masculine *logos*, as better than wisdom, or the feminine *Sophia*. The preference for *logos* over *Sophia* also leads to a male Jesus. Jesus is understood as the *word* of God; as Scripture states, "in the beginning was the Word, and the Word was with God, and the Word was God" (John 1:1).

Thus, Christianity has a long patriarchal history, and the maleness of Jesus further reinforces patriarchy, dominance, and white supremacy. If the church today emphasizes a white Jesus, the congregation will believe in a white Jesus. A white Jesus reinforces whiteness in the congregation and Christianity as a whole.

EUROPEAN ART REINFORCES A WHITE JESUS

The earliest depictions of Jesus emerged in the first through third centuries CE. These images were less concerned about accurately reflecting Jesus' appearance and more focused on clarifying Jesus' role as a ruler and a savior. By the fifth century, under Roman Emperor Constantine, who had converted to Christianity, depictions of Jesus increased but were more and more white, with brown hair, a beard, and even a halo. The European artists gave Jesus European features and lighter skin to connect themselves to Jesus.[6] It was almost a projection of themselves upon Jesus and was the opposite of God's command to not "make any for yourselves an idol" (Exodus 20:4). The movement to create a more European Jesus was a very intentional tactic to establish a deity that looked like them and made them closer to Jesus than people of color. It resulted in reinforcing white people's power and privilege and kept nonwhites subjugated and subordinated.

In the sixth century, Byzantine artists began portraying a white-skinned, blue-eyed Jesus with light hair—the image that prevails today and will continue to be accepted as long as whiteness remains within the church and Christian faith. These paintings misportrayed and misinformed people of faith that Jesus is white. By the Middle Ages, the Roman Empire had been replaced with papal authority during the crusades. There was continual fighting between European Christians and Middle Eastern Muslims. To white Christians, the nonwhite nonbelievers were the enemy. Even though Jesus looked more like the Middle Eastern people than Europeans, for the crusaders, it was important to uphold the image of Jesus as a white man. They could not and would not paint Jesus like their enemy. It put God on the side of the colonizers and dominators.[7] And there was an utmost urgency to solidify the perception of Jesus as a white man with light features.

An important part of dismantling this wrong perception is remembering the social contexts that created a white male Jesus,

which helps us understand the reasons for the continual misrep-
resentation of Jesus as a white European man.

Da Vinci's *Last Supper* further misconstrued the perception of
Jesus by portraying his last supper with him seated on a European
chair in front of a standing dining table. This was not how people
ate during the time of Jesus. Rather, they would have been re-
clining on the floor around a low-rise dining table. Now this
popular image is embedded in the minds of Christians. For much
of my life I thought this was an accurate portrayal of Jesus' last
supper. I never questioned it and innocently and wholeheartedly
accepted it as the truth.

Michelangelo's *Last Judgment* also depicts a white European
judgment story. I visited the Sistine Chapel with my children
when they were younger, and I was astounded by the majestic
beauty. I marveled at the magnificent painting. Yet while the
crafting of it is awe-inspiring, it is a harmful contribution to the
whitewashing of Jesus.

WHITE JESUS IN INDIA

The deep impact and legacy of white missionary work is still evident today in India. During my seminary studies, I spent a
summer there through a missionary program for students with
the Presbyterian Church in Canada. It was a scorching hot
summer in 1990, and the discomfort of the heat was nothing like
I had ever experienced in my life. My second day in India, I was
so hot that all I kept thinking of was the biblical story of Daniel
and his friends being tossed into the furnace. To me, India was
the fiery furnace I was thrown into for three months. After a week
in India, my body slowly acclimated, and I felt I would be able to
survive the unbearable summer heat. I spent time in New Delhi,
Agra, and Calcutta with white Presbyterian women missionaries.

In all of these cities, I visited different schools, churches, and households to teach Scripture and help the missionaries who were running schools and community centers. I was there mostly as a missionary assistant and did whatever odd jobs they needed done, such as indexing schoolbooks.

As I visited the various schools, churches, and homes I noticed a familiar picture of a white Jesus hanging on the walls. It was the all-too-recognizable print my mother had. I was a bit stunned to see this familiar image halfway across the world in India. But in a way, the presence of Sallman's image in India confirmed for me at that time that this image of Jesus was the real portrait of Jesus. This white Jesus picture in India helped the British colonizers convey the goodness of the British people. The underlying message was that if Jesus the savior was white, the British who were also white would be India's savior. It legitimized British colonization as a way to civilize and bring economic prosperity to Indians, concealing colonial evil and suffering. If Jesus was white, then the whiteness the British were bringing must be good.

All these churches and mission compounds were run by white missionaries from North America or Europe, and they taught of a white Jesus and a white God. The churches and even the artwork hanging inside the churches were European and white. Young girls and women went to church with a white lace veil or handkerchief over their heads. This is what the white missionaries told them to do, and they followed their instructions. This covering of their heads with white lace underscored the purity and cleanliness of white.

The white Jesus was intentionally contrived to serve white men who were in power and wanted to continue to hold that power globally.

WEAPONIZING JESUS' WHITENESS

One of white supremacy's most powerful myths—the idea of a white Jesus—quietly solved white people's moral and practical dilemmas. White Jesus essentially made enslavement legitimate because, if Jesus was white, then it was right for white people to do what they wanted. Jesus' whiteness excused white people's enslavement of nonwhites.[8] Whiteness is not just a category of people; rather it is a powerful concept that forms and impacts our thoughts, practices, and behaviors. Whiteness affects culture, politics, and religion and the various laws and doctrines that organize such entities.

The whiteness of Jesus became the architecture of white supremacy. A white Jesus was used to colonize countries around the world, engage in holy wars, and enforce enslavement and indentured servitude and genocide. Countless evils were committed in the name of a white Jesus and constructed and maintained by this white Jesus. The destructive power of whiteness is real. It is overpowering and makes people of color feel illegitimate and marginalized.

When I was teaching in a seminary, white male students gave me trouble for teaching theology. A woman of color teaching theology was foreign and unacceptable to some white students, and they were suspicious of me. They felt my teachings weren't legitimate or even truthful because I was trying to assert myself as a woman of color in a white man's world. One day, a student approached me in the hallway outside of my office and said, "I have nothing to learn from a woman or a person of color." This dagger crushed my heart. I had been struggling to become a better professor, and this so affected me that I became depressed and anxious. It was a dreadful moment in my teaching career. But it doesn't stop with one confrontational statement. Even if unsaid, there is a pervasive sentiment that exists in the seminary buildings, classrooms, hallways, and even in our churches.

The prominence of whiteness has been wedded to Christianity from its beginnings, and it is extremely difficult to divorce the two, as there is much resistance from those in power to do so. But they desperately need to be separated, otherwise white Christianity will continue to be damaging and problematic, and more and more people of color will be destroyed in the name of God.

COLORBLINDNESS IS BLINDNESS

Colorblindness is a stance used by white people to declare that race doesn't matter. The argument prevents white people from reckoning with the truth that race actually does matter to everyone, including white people. Whiteness matters to white people, otherwise they would be willing to work to eradicate it. Whites who choose to advocate for colorblindness as the cure for racism or as a way to deny their own racism do not recognize that this doesn't solve the root issue and only appears progressive. In effect, it sustains white supremacy. Most whites do not make racist comments or violate the rules of political correctness. However, whites want to preserve white advantages through the denial of racial differences. Many well-meaning whites tell themselves, "I don't see color. Like Martin Luther King Jr., I do not judge people by the color of their skin but by the content of their character. I treat everyone the same!"[9] In doing so, they declare race to be meaningless and not a category used to judge people or create laws. But colorblindness is dangerous because white people use it to cover up their own racism and racist attitudes with a simple phrase.

Even if we accept the myth that an individual does not see color, social structures are designed to see color for them and act

accordingly. Were we to call for a truly colorblind society and establish an absolutely level playing field, white people would be up
in arms. Social structures continue to privilege whites despite
whites' claims concerning colorblindness.[10] Creating a colorblind
society is impossible, as racism is already embedded in society.

White people wonder why everyone can't be treated the same
while simultaneously ignoring how social structures have been
historically designed to benefit them. As they argue for colorblindness, they make Jesus white and do not see the negative
consequences that follow.

DISMANTLING WHITE CHRISTIANITY

White Christianity claims to seek racial harmony and reconciliation, but it is only possible through a personal relationship with
their white Jesus who they say can move across all racial and
ethnic lines.[11] The problem is that Jesus was never white, and the
suggestion that he can reach all people regardless of race is incon-
sistent with the fact that they robbed him of his true race to make
him conform to their ideals.

They tell people of color that everyone who makes the white
Jesus their Lord and savior can become brothers and sisters, regardless of their race or ethnicity. But it requires people of color
assimilate into whiteness. Personal piety over and against societal changes provides a false sense of righteousness that never
needs to examine its complicity with racist structures. Such argu-
ments, wishing to preserve white advantages through the denial
of racial differences, prevent any hope of liberation among the
marginalized. In this system, white people's privileges are more
important than any form of liberation for the oppressed. This in
its very premise goes against the message of Jesus who came to
free the oppressed and set them free. White Christians who offer

reconciliatory rhetoric while remaining unwilling to give up any of the benefits of whiteness cannot be allowed to define the terms of racial reconciliation. Setting the terms for racial reconciliation must fall on the shoulders of those on the underside of society, those yearning for justice. Their struggle becomes the grassroots context from which any meaningful discussion of reconciliation must arise, a reconciliation based on the pursuit of salvation and liberation.[12] Reconciliation begins with the oppressed, not the oppressor. This conversation and action must be directed by those experiencing the pain of racial injustice as a result of up-holding a white Christianity and a white Jesus. This task is long overdue and is urgent. The voices of the marginalized and the oppressed need to be uplifted to reverse the damages caused by Christian whiteness.

In the course of Christian history, having a white male Jesus helped unify Christians and helped solidify white male leadership in the church. It reinforced the status quo within the church leadership and kept the peace within church and society. Whiteness reinforced white people's power over people of color, and a white male Jesus only extenuated white people's power. A white male Jesus helped enforce enslavement of Africans. Using a white male Jesus validated the goodness and authority of white people. A white Jesus represented purity, white superiority, and whiteness. Any other Jesus would have challenged the dominion of white masters.

To overcome white supremacy, it is essential that we acknowledge it, name it, and understand its origins. We need to call out evil and work toward dismantling the systems that perpetuate racism, prejudice, and xenophobia. Black theology has been doing this as they depict a Black Jesus who saves and frees them. James Cone, the father of Black theology, has been writing on the God of the oppressed and has written about a Black Jesus who liberates Black communities and people of color. For many communities of color, a white Jesus is often associated with white supremacy and white power. Some Hispanic communities have embraced a dark Jesus who is present in poor neighborhoods and is for the poor and oppressed communities of color.

In Korea, Minjung theology, which means "people and mass," speaks out against oppressive political regimes such as military dictators during the 1980s who were killing, arresting, and silencing people who spoke out against the military regime. Minjung theologians resorted to an East Asian depiction of Jesus who was with the poor, the oppressed, and the outcasts of society. I have visited a minjung church during my travel to Korea and was moved by how the church cares for the poor and the marginalized in Korean society. Minjung churches exist in poor communities and help with free daycare for poor families and other services that are not readily available in the poorer communities. They focus on a liberating Jesus who is not associated with the powerful military and oppressive regimes.

We need to deconstruct this obscene reality of the past white Christianity and work toward a more faithful and liberative understanding of Christianity and God. We must work toward freedom and a life of equality and equity so everyone is welcomed to the banquet table that God has prepared for us.

7

A WHITE GOD

Our family had no religious affiliation when we first landed in Canada; but, traditionally, our family in Korea was Buddhist. The small Korean immigrant community in Canada was very tight, and most of us lived in the poorer area of town in small apartment buildings. Many of the Koreans who immigrated to North America in the 1970s were young families in search of a brighter future than a war-torn country struggling to survive economically could provide. Many of the young families were financially unstable due to lower economic standards of living in Korea. Naturally, as Korean immigrants lived close together in these poorer areas, they developed friendships and treated one another like family.

The Korean immigrant community started a few churches. Through peer pressure, they invited each other to church. Some families didn't really want to attend, but since it was an opportunity to build community, many went anyway. The Korean Presbyterian church my family attended was more of a social club for the first few years before my parents started to have faith in the Christian God.

Korean immigrant churches were poor, so we worshiped in rented church buildings, which meant our Sunday worship services were held on Sunday afternoons. There was always a Korean meal to follow the service. It seemed as though most of the day revolved around church. We gathered in the morning to prepare food, practice choir, and get things ready for service. Once a month, there was a district or small group Bible study meeting on a Saturday night or a Sunday evening. If it landed on a Sunday evening, I spent the whole Sunday at church and church activities.

Once my parents saw the value of attending church, they became very excited about church. There they built friendships, learned about Canadian society and culture, and educated their kids in the Korean language. Church became a multipurpose community that functioned as an employment center, an education center, a counseling center, and a place of worship. It was everything wrapped up into one community, which was very beneficial to the immigrant family. My dad thought the Korean as well as non-Korean churches were great for my sister and me, so he sent us to several churches throughout the week.

When I was a child, there was no doubt in my mind that God was a white man. In my faith and church community, there was no space for a nonwhite God, as it was the white church leaders who reinforced this false notion of God. Like Koreans in Korea, I as a child of immigrants wholeheartedly embraced whiteness and a white male God who was almighty, superior, and all powerful. This was the God we learned about in white churches as well as my Korean church. White supremacy and the notion that white is best were ingrained into my very being, and to challenge it was against my upbringing and morals.

My family was very conservative, just like the other Korean immigrant families. Korean immigrant churches just retaught and re-preached the same white gospel message that the white missionaries taught them back in Korea. There was no adaptation, modification, or translation of the good news into the Korean immigrant context. It was simply a direct translation of a white male gospel that traveled from America to Korea and then back to Korean immigrant families in North America.

Growing up in the church, it never occurred to me that there was a direct link between racism and the white God we learned about. As a child, I didn't understand or believe that a white God perpetuates racism, and racism reinforces a white God. Today the obvious connectedness and interrelatedness between whiteness and a white God is clear to me. These two concepts feed off one another and sustains each other to the detriment of people of color and women.

I became heavily indoctrinated in a white male God during worship, Bible study, fellowship, hymns, and Bible game time at all the other churches I attended during the week. This was the white male God reality in which I grew up.

KEEPING THE FAITH

My sister and I decided to take our families on a European cruise one summer. This cruise went to different ports in Europe along the Mediterranean where we could disembark and spend the day in different cities. We visited places I had always dreamed of visiting like Pompeii, which I had read about in elementary school, and the Leaning Tower of Pisa, which I had only seen in movies. We also visited Rome and Vatican City where we explored the incredible Colosseum and made wishes at the beautiful Trevi Fountain. Then we toured the breathtaking Sistine Chapel, and I was mesmerized by the overwhelmingly beautiful ceiling. It was spectacular, tremendous, awe-inspiring . . . and yet patriarchal. The ceiling portrayed God as an old white man with a white beard. It was exactly as I had been taught in Sunday school.

Michelangelo painted scenes from the book of Genesis to depict the creation story with Adam, and Eve, and three stories of Noah. In these scenes, God is painted as a powerful white male. The most famous scene in the painting is of the creation of Adam, a picture that is ingrained in people globally whether they are Christian or not.

The paradox of art is that it is an expression of our thoughts and desires, and, in turn, artwork influences our thoughts and desires. Michelangelo and other Christians at that time didn't question the imagery of a white male God, and people still don't today. God is understood to be a powerful deity, and power is associated with men. To be powerful like God, we must emulate white male strength.

I saw many other drawings and artwork that clearly depicted an old white man as God. I saw them in Sunday school and in children's books. At that time, there was not a doubt in my mind that these images were real, earthly depictions of the divine. I was socially and religiously conditioned to accept white people's teaching as the truth.

In Korean churches in Korea and in the diaspora, it is very common to address God as Father God or heavenly Father (*Ha Na Nhim A-bu-gi*). Koreans learned about this Father God from the white missionaries when they arrived in Korea, and it stayed with them when the missionaries left.

Prayers would contain the phrase Father God (*Ha Na Nhim A-bu-gi*) multiple times in one sentence. It felt like a mantra that people said over and over again in prayers and liturgies. Growing up in the church, I would hear this phrase used frequently throughout a prayer by the male minister during the Sunday morning worship service. It was also used often during times of testimony, Bible study classes, and fellowship. *Ha Na Nhim*

A-bu-gi was so ingrained in my mind that it left me no room to believe in a God who could be feminine.

As discussed earlier in this book, words, phrases, and language used to talk about God or to address God are all mere metaphors. We cannot fully comprehend the infinite God that we are worshiping, praying to, and believing in. Since words matter, the phrase *Ha Na Nhim A-bu-gi* can be limiting to our understanding of God. That tied in with the image of a white God as presented by the white missionaries who came to Korea can be constraining and have significant consequences. It can limit our perceptions not only of God but of ourselves.

I now see the big problem with the whiteness of God. It can prevent an Asian American woman like myself from seeing oneself as being fully created in the image of God. Further, it prevents white people from accepting people of color as equal and fully made in the image of God. In religion, our beliefs and understandings are reduced to words and actions. Words define and then convey what we really believe whether in conversations, study groups, or worship. In the past, where art, images, icons, sculptures, and stained-glass windows provided teachings and biblical understanding, presently words are the key to religious behavior.

That is why words, and the way we deploy them, are so important. In Christianity, words are one of the few tools we have to make sense of the faith we cling to. If we keep talking about whiteness and the whiteness of God, it damages the rest of us who are not white, placing us at a lower rung in the hierarchy. This ultimately leads to white supremacy.

Asians make up 60 percent of the world's population. We are the majority of the world's people, but white supremacy has continued to subordinate us and make us feel less valued than white Europeans. In the United States, I am racialized, minoritized, and marginalized, even though I am part of a people who make up 60 percent of the world. How Asians and Asian Americans view and understand God is important, and we need to reimagine God in more inclusive ways.

PRAYING TO A WHITE GOD

Koreans like to pray. Koreans like to pray in many different ways. Praying out loud and in public is almost a ritual and a display of personal piety. In public worship, they like to pray corporate prayer or *tong-son-gido*. This is a type of prayer where the minister will say, "Let us pray out loud," and then everyone in the sanctuary will pray their own prayers out loud at the same time. Some will be yelling and some will be mumbling next to you. I grew up with *tong-son-gido*, and at times it would scare me. People would start yelling out prayers or saying their prayers as if it was a shouting match. Some prayed so loud that I couldn't concentrate on my own prayers or even say a prayer myself. However, it was my mother's preferred way of praying, and she believed it was the best way to pray. My mother was the quietest and most timid person I knew. But when it came to *tong-son-gido,* she became another person. She prayed, mostly about my sister and me doing well in school, with outstretched arms and tears in her eyes. It was a sacred moment for her to engage in *tong-son-gido* and no one could take it away from her. In Korean churches, many worshipers cry out *Ha Na Nhim A-bu-gi* in their prayers. Even as the minister is praying, many will say *Ha Na Nhim A-bu-gi* under their breath to affirm what the minister is praying.

This *tong-son-gido* is the exact opposite of the Presbyterian Church worship prayers that I participate in today. As a pulpit supply minister, I preach in different Presbyterian churches, and the prayers are tame, quiet, and prayed by the minister or recited in unison as printed in the church bulletin. The prayer is never prayed out loud by individual worshipers or screamed out loud by a minister. For Korean Christians, there is no doubt that God is a white male God and the *tong-son-gido* shows this reality as they publicly and loudly address God as a heavenly Father with the implication that God is white. This is what the white missionaries taught them when they came to bring the good news. But Koreans did not realize the consequences of this white male God delivered by the white missionaries. They did not recognize that it would affirm white is best and that if Koreans immigrated to other parts of the world like Europe and North America, they would be experiencing racism, xenophobia, discrimination, and subordination due to the color of other skin. Now, after a long history of such teachings that God is white, it is difficult for Koreans to rid themselves of the teaching of white superiority. This is the power of whiteness. The portrayal of whiteness as good and necessary becomes so ingrained in one's culture, understanding, and psyche that it is difficult to extricate this whiteness.

As a result, the power of whiteness gets transferred to our understanding of God, and the white male God has become so embedded in our belief and faith system that many would rather suffer the consequences of imagining and believing in a white male God instead of challenge this long-standing belief. Many Korean immigrants will suffer in silence rather than challenge the whiteness of God.

THE PROBLEM OF A WHITE MALE GOD

Mary Daly said, "If God is male, then the male is God."[1] We can update this saying in light of whiteness and say, "If God is a white male, then the white male is God." Seeing white men as gods means that anyone who is not white or male falls short of divinity. Women will forever be viewed as inferior and ill-equipped to do God's work faithfully and diligently on earth. The whiteness of God is created by white men, which in turn elevates them to become like God. White man wants the rest of us to worship him, lay our gifts before his feet, bow down to him, and lift him up in society.

A white male God reinforces and legitimizes patriarchy and white supremacy. It is a ruse to perpetuate white European power, wealth, prominence, and colonialism.

People of color can never be valued and accepted as long as white is considered the ideal. The perception that people of color don't achieve anything on their own merit is perpetuated by the misunderstanding of what affirmative action is designed to accomplish. This unjust narrative follows people of color wherever we go from schools to workplaces and into our contributions to society. We are always under suspicion and must work twice as hard to get any recognition.

In July 2009, Harvard scholar Dr. Henry Louis Gates was arrested for disorderly conduct as he was trying to enter his own home. His door was jammed, and a woman called the police because she thought a Black man was breaking into a home. The cops came and he was arrested, handcuffed, and held in a cell for four hours. Dr. Gates, a prominent scholar, was viewed as a robber while a white man doing the same thing would have gone unnoticed.

On February 26, 2012, a seventeen-year-old African American boy, Trayvon Martin, was shot dead by George Zimmerman while walking home to his father's fiancée's townhouse in Sanford, Florida. The life of this young, innocent Black boy was taken because he was perceived as being in the wrong neighborhood. In May 2020, George Floyd was not just killed by police, but he was brutalized for being Black. It was a modern-day lynching. And in 2023, we are reeling over the horrifying assault on Tyre Nichols in Memphis. These and countless more stories of people of color being attacked demonstrate an ongoing problem with violence being tolerated because people of color are not viewed as entirely human or created in the image of God. A white God does not make room for them to be considered equal.

The perception of Black people as evil is even embedded in our pop culture and literature. In the Star Wars movie franchise, the good people are white and Darth Vader, who is the prominent evil character, is dressed in black from head to toe.[2] This pervading imagery of black being bad and white being good perpetuates racism, prejudice, and stereotyping of Black people and other people of color, both implicitly and explicitly. The list of examples of the stereotyping and racist acts that are happening in our society against people of color goes on and on.

CHURCH-SANCTIONED RACISM

Churches across the United States have a long historical legacy and participation in racist teachings and practices. The Southern Baptist Convention began in 1845 when it split from northern Baptists over enslavement. Both northern and southern Methodists held that Black Methodists had a subservient place in society. Despite United Methodist support for civil rights, most white Methodists in the South supported white supremacist practices. Additionally, the Roman Catholic Church has long reinforced colonialism in Africa and the Global South by teaching that white Christians were chosen by God to civilize the rest of the world, and maintained slavery in the eighteenth- and nineteenth-century United States.[3] Looking back at history reveals how white Christian churches were complacent and complicit in failing to challenge racism. Instead, they were part of maintaining racial structures of white supremacy.

White Christians have maintained their undeserved power and privilege through violence on bodies of color. Ironically, they have demanded that a more just society must occur nonviolently and according to a plan controlled by and within their oversight. White Christians fail to see how their positions are obtained by institutionalized violence. Their white political structures are damaging communities and killing communities of color. White Christian nationalists teach that Jesus loved peace, but they lift up a Jesus who loves to fight as hymns of soldiers, blood, and sacrifice are continuously sung in worship.[4] They continuously contradict themselves as they preach peace and nonviolence, reminding communities of color that they can obtain liberation only through peaceful means and if they achieve it violently, they are awful, mentally ill people who should be thrown in jail or institutionalized.

Christians who are pacifists still unintentionally go against people of color as they exist in this system of whiteness, which continues to privilege their worldview and interests. Therefore, out of ignorance, they can become complicit in white supremacy and white privilege. However, white pacifists can move forward to dismantle white Christianity by recognizing their own complicity and the need to name it and challenge it themselves. White pacifists hold a lot of power, and they need to channel their power toward good and stand in solidarity with people of color as they work in dismantling white Christianity. White allies such as Jim Wallis, the founder and editor of *Sojourners Magazine,* have been fighting racism and standing in solidarity with people of color. Tony Campolo and Shane Claiborne, the founders of Red Letter Christians, have been white allies as they speak out against systemic racism. Their solidarity with the people of color community has been helpful in fighting against Christian white nationalism and the killing of innocent Black men by police officers.

There are various ways that Christians react to white supremacy in the church. Some donate their money to fight racism or just view it from afar. Some rely on missionaries to fix the problem of racism.[5] However, many white people do not recognize the problem that white missionaries have caused for people around the globe. They have harmed countless people through cultural genocide, casting themselves in the role of savior. White missionaries claim to protect and save these "savages" from evils and bring them to a white male God who will provide eternal life. Whiteness introduces a false narrative in which there is a hierarchy of people, and white people live at the top. White Christianity allows racism to seep into the church among leaders and church members.

The greater problem is the denial that racism exists, or if it does exist it's only in the extreme forms of lynchings, cross burnings, and racial slurs and epithets. This is systemic, and it is embedded in how our society functions. One of the problems in not properly identifying and acknowledging the many forms of racism in our society is that we overlook or diminish the experiences of some groups facing this discrimination and abuse.

White identity is defined by what it isn't: Blackness.[6] This dichotomy has positioned racism as largely Black versus white. The problem here isn't just that one group of people is elevated over another; it's that if you are a person of color but not Black, then your experiences may not be considered racism. The people of color who fall between this Black and white dichotomy—Latinx, Asian Americans, Native Americans—get lost in this misconception. When Asian Americans voice their experiences of marginalization and oppression, they are often told that it can't be racism since they are not Black.

White Americans often tell Asian Americans that because we are "honorary whites" our experiences aren't "real" racism. But limiting the conversation on racism to such oversimplified terms diminishes the crucial damage it does to all people of color. Racism as a Black versus white conversation negates the prejudice, stereotyping, and hurt that other groups of people have experienced.[7] We must move away from these either-or terms. White privilege succeeds when people of color are in tension with each other. And that is exactly what happens when myths are perpetuated about certain minorities—myths such as the one that says Asian Americans are "model minorities." The "model minority" myth tells other people of color to stop complaining; if they "just work a little bit harder," they can succeed like Asian Americans. This is a false narrative and mitigates the real problem for those who don't want to acknowledge it.[8]

Not only does the church appease the guilt and individual responsibility by finding biblical justification, it simply pretends it doesn't exist.

LEAVING BEHIND A WHITE GOD

My mother's biggest concern was prayer and sharing her love for Christ with her two daughters. She taught me to pray, fast, and pray some more. She would lock herself in her room and pray. Sometimes she would even speak in tongues. Mind you, we lived in a tiny two-bedroom apartment, so when my mother prayed in tongues in her tiny bedroom, I thought the entire apartment was going to cave in.

Everything my mother taught me came from the teachings passed on in the Korean seminaries to the ordained male Korean pastors who then crossed the ocean and became pastors in North America. What they brought with them was the white Christianity of the missionaries delivered to them when they came to Korea just one hundred years prior. These Korean Christians inherited a white Christianity, and that is what they passed on to the next generation of believers.

People tend to fashion God and Jesus as white—pure and good. A white Christ didn't only justify enslavement of the dark, evil people, it went further and declared a strong announcement about who God is and who God favors. As Christ became portrayed more and more like a white man, it was assumed that God must care more about white people's context, experiences, hardships, and problems than Black people's enduring of hardships, enslavement, lynchings, and sufferings.[9] The center of Christianity and God was white. This implied that whites are the center of humanity. God's concerns and God's desires centered and focused on white people. The church believed God was more concerned about privileged white people than anyone else—they were the true chosen people and the preferred better race. The rest of us people of color are on the sidelines and are secondary to white people.

This is significant as it sheds new light and understanding to people of color who were experiencing grave injustices due to racism, discrimination, and xenophobia. The white Jesus revealed and reinforced a white God who prioritized white people and who was not troubled by people of color's suffering and oppression. This was a way to prove that God was not concerned about enslavement of Blacks, genocide of Native Americans, indenturing of Asian Americans, or the oppression of Latinx community. Therefore, there was no reason to end or abolish any form of oppression toward people of color. In this manner, God became clearly associated with white supremacy. As a result, all the injustice associated with it was now deeply legitimized through a white God.

We need to grapple with the reality that the Christian God has become a white God. Even though the Ten Commandments clearly state not to worship any graven images, throughout

Christian history, humanity has created God in our own image, and this has profound consequences on the rest of society and the church. By creating a white male God, white supremacy and white male privilege gets reinforced by the entire Christian institution.

The Bible teaches us to love everyone and that everyone is created by God and created in the image of God. We are all to be kind to all people regardless of our differences. But we have limited God's commandment to love our neighbors and made it very selective. We only love those who are like us. The message of "good news" has been tainted with pervasive subliminal signaling that white is best.

Loving one another should have no exceptions—not sexual orientation, gender identity, ethnicity, religion, ableism, or economic lifestyle. But this seems to be problematic in Christianity as whiteness has a lingering influence over who we are to love and who we are to hate.

Dispossessed communities believe and live into the lie of white supremacy, which pushes them to the margins as white Christianity lives in and with racism.[10] This is how white supremacy exists within religion and indoctrinates adherents with the message that people of color are lesser. As a result, white people get to define God and create a religion to benefit themselves. With a white superiority complex, it becomes very easy to destroy, enslave, and conquer others. The genocide of Native Americans has nearly destroyed a people who were living in North America for thousands of years. In order for the white church to truly embody love and share the good news to all people it must acknowledge the problem of whiteness within the church. Unless there is acknowledgment of its evil past and present ways, there is no way to move forward.

As a mother of three children, a theology professor, and an ordained minister, I have had some time to reflect on my Christian upbringing and the disconnect between what I was taught and my own experiences of living as an Asian American in a white society. All of my encounters with racism challenge the core of my mother's teachings and the white Christianity I grew up with. I have faced an ongoing challenge reconciling what I have experienced and seen of racism with what I have been taught about God and Christianity. It is a problem worth investigating and discussing as we need to change the course of history. We need to see how we can become better informed and better Christians. Only by understanding our Christian history and heritage will we identify the trajectory and understand how to move toward a different future.

Through the invention of a white Jesus and a white male God, the reality of a white Christian empire is steeped in problems, the impact of which has spread throughout the world. Jesus was an olive-skinned Palestinian Jew living under an empire. But Jesus didn't accept the Roman Empire. Rather, he challenged it by teaching and showing another kind of possibility,[11] the kin-dom of love, justice, and equality. Today, white Christians need to engage in racial justice work to reverse the damages of a white Christianity, a white Jesus, and a white male God. We need to challenge the white male Christian empire and work toward an all-embracing and all-loving kin-dom of God.

8

THE PROBLEM OF A WHITE
GENDERED GOD

Korean immigrant churches love to eat after worship service. It isn't just donuts and coffee, but a real sit-down meal, as eating is a communal and almost necessary fellowship. Koreans feel that if there is no food, there isn't any point in gathering. They commonly greet one another by asking, "Have you eaten?" Eating is a vital part of the culture that brings families and friends together in a loving bond. Food is a love language between mothers and their children. Food is so important that even weddings revolve around eating, and many will say they are going to a wedding just to eat. Funerals and ancestor worship are also meal-centric. In a world of social media and online videos, Koreans love to create and watch *mukbang*, which are online eating shows where a host consumes food on an audiovisual broadcast. This simple show of a person eating food which may not sound very entertaining, has actually become very popular in 2010 and has become a global trend.

However, not all meal celebrations were positive for me growing up. When I was twelve years old two older men started arguing about the pastor's sermon during lunch after the worship service. Both men suddenly stood up from their chairs and started yelling at each other. Hands and arms started flying, and one man took his bowl of Korean bone broth soup and rice and threw it at the other man. I was in shock to see what was unfolding right before my eyes.

As the bowl was hurled into the air, women raced out of the kitchen to clean up the mess. They hurried around the two arguing men and wiped off the food from one man and wiped the hands of the other man. One woman brought out a trash bin and another a mop and yet another woman some wipes to clean off the table. I couldn't believe my eyes as the men just sat around while the women were running around cleaning up their mess. Two men behaved badly and created a big mess, yet it was the women who rushed from whatever they were doing in the kitchen to clean it up. It became very clear for me at that moment that it was a man's world at church. This shocking fight incident left a deep pain in my young self. I knew this could not be accepted as a just order in society or church, and something needed to change.

Patriarchy has always been part of the church, and it is still rampant in our contemporary churches. Women stay in the kitchen and cook long hours while men sit in meetings and make decisions and are waited on hand and foot. This form of sexism and patriarchy is legitimized and reinforced by a white male God who ordered the universe and also the church under patriarchy. Men have power and women are to be obedient, subordinate to men, and subservient.

Growing up in the church, I only saw male leadership and male ministers. All the ministers I ever met, saw on television, or heard on the radio were men. I had no exposure to or encounters with any women pastors or leaders in the church. There was no question in the Korean church that men preach and lead while women remain silent and serve in the kitchen, nursery school, or

Sunday school. Later, when I attended non-Korean churches, I found a similar scenario—no women ministers or leaders in the church. It was all run by men.

HISTORY OF PATRIARCHY IN RELIGION

I grew up in a patriarchal household, a model that was passed down through generations. My paternal grandfather didn't know how to take care of my grandmother, so he often resorted to violence to control her and punish her if he felt she did something wrong. Despite physical abuse, my grandmother suffered in silence. My father witnessed this domestic violence when he was growing up, and as an old man, he still talks about the fear he had when his father lost his temper and started to throw things around the tiny house and was physically and verbally abusive to his mother. This kind of abuse, violence, and damage to women and children is permissible in a patriarchal society. Furthermore, in some patriarchal societies, this type of violence toward the vulnerable is upheld as macho, and manly. Some men would even brag about how they kept their woman in line by using force or inducing some kind of fear in them.

Patriarchy is embedded in the historical, cultural, and religious practices in society. This long history of patriarchy has influenced how we view the divine, how we view the world, and how we treat one another. A patriarchal notion and masculine perception of the divine has negatively influenced how women are viewed and valued in society. In a patriarchal society, the more powerful a man becomes, the more the woman is weakened.[1] Patriarchy works to lower women and to diminish their power. Man uses his power to keep woman in her place.

Scripture was interpreted, read, and used to create divisions between genders, races, ages, cultures, and continents. Feminist writer bell hooks described patriarchy as a political-social system that insists that men are inherently dominating, superior to all things, and women are weak. Men are endowed with the right to dominate and rule over the weak (women) and to maintain their power through various forms of psychological terrorism and violence.[2] It is the corollary of how white people treat people of color, and it demonstrates the intersectionality of how oppression works and is maintained.

The concept of deity emerged quite early during human development, as early Stone Age cave paintings and artifacts reveal. Deities in early Stone Age artwork reflect projections of the human being's sense of a reality and presence that is beyond their own immediate understanding and context. Early human beings somehow had a sense of a deity who was separate and beyond themselves. They made use of the natural elements in their environment and their own experience of existence to communicate with the deity. The specific shapes and concepts applied to the deity have been based on the highest form that human beings can conceive of themselves. Humans created deities in animal guise and other elements from creation, but the deities always had some humanlike component. History notes that while no human has ever seen God, man has continuously formed deities in his own image. God was portrayed like human beings in appearance, thought, and speech, and in the world they created. Procreative gods and goddesses reflected a sense of superiority based on an assumption that human beings out of all the animals are the only ones who can make creation conscious of itself. They do this by projecting their own life experiences onto a cave wall, in a musical work, in a painting, or on the concept of deity itself.[3]

Human beings conceived the divine in their own image and in most cases have attributed maleness to God. This attribution of gender to the divine has limited the divine, has tied them to our reproductive cycles, and even imposed our own death-defined experience. In the study of world religions, very few religions or mythologies embrace a genderless deity.[4] Most conceptions of God are gendered and are conceived and manifested in a patriarchal framework. This gendered God has made a huge impact on society. If early human beings viewed God as masculine, then men are viewed and accepted as superior to women because men are more like God than women are. This history of a gendered male God is further revealed in the long legacy of women as the sinner, the subjugated, and the other, while men are the ruler, the dominator, and the powerful.

It is not just the whiteness of God that is problematic but also the gendering of God as a man. These two identities of whiteness and maleness that were cast on the Christian God have influenced church doctrines, liturgy, prayer, hermeneutics, and the life of the church. This gendered God is emphasized in the Old Testament as well as in the New Testament. Male pronouns and nouns have been used throughout the Scriptures to describe and refer to God. It is strange that throughout church history, strong patriarchal words such as *King, Master, Lord, Sovereign,* and *Almighty* are used to talk about a loving and graceful God. In light of sexism, gendered violence, and other atrocities committed against women in society and in Christianity, this white gendered understanding of God is clearly problematic.

A gendered God legitimizes and promotes patriarchy and discrimination, and it subordinates and problematizes women in church and society. When racism and sexism intersect, women of color—especially Black women—endure the greatest hardships and atrocities.

Women live in a world where men push them to assume the status of the other, and they have become subjugated in society, family, and under religion. This dynamic is demonstrated in various spheres of society and in relationships such as in traditional marriages, family relationships, and the church where men have power over women.

To make women into an other benefits men greatly. Simone de Beauvoir believes that men view woman as a sexual partner, a reproducer, an erotic object—an other through whom he seeks himself. Women have been objectified by men throughout centuries in many cultures and societies. As objects, women can be violated, abused, and sexually assaulted without any fear of repercussion. In our world where so much of our existence is cast in dualistic terms, the division this creates prevents us from being able to embrace hybridity, ambiguity, and trans identity.

Woman as the other means there is not a reciprocal relation between man and woman. Women are still treated as property, and the autonomy women supposedly have in a marriage or family is illusory. A woman's place is whatever a man assigns to her,[5] as she is the other and has no agency. Even in Christianity, women are the other and are treated as such. We see this during biblical times, in the early church, and throughout church history to the present day.

INTERSECTIONALITY

We cannot seem to rid ourselves of this entrenched notion of patriarchy in society and in religion. Religion is a powerful force in our society, and it can have devastating effects on women if religion is gone unchecked. Christianity has become so white and westernized that anything non-Western sounds foreign, untrue, or even evil. As a result, we cannot talk about sexism without talking about racism. These issues are interrelated and intersectional. Sexism does not work alone in oppressing women. Sexism works with racism, ethnic discrimination, homophobia, trans-phobia, and classism to oppress women. These issues are not distinct categories operating in isolated compartments but are all interconnected. There are sexist-based paradigms which attempt to domesticate and dominate all women and people of color. Sexism, as a form of oppression, is as much about racism and classism as it is about gender oppression.

In patriarchy, white men are endowed by their white creator to dominate people of color and women. The toxic masculinity and whiteness fulfills white males' need for supremacy and power. This is often ignored or dismissed as many people of color are indoctrinated into male white Christianity and do not see their own source of oppression. Inferiority is engraved in our bodies as we are stripped of power or agency and become subjugated to patriarchy.[6] Issues of hegemony and racism intersect to continue oppression.

PATRIARCHAL CHRISTIANITY

Sexism is embedded in the church, and many in the church do not seem to question or challenge it. Many churches use biblical passages to this day to back up sexism. For example: "Women should be silent in the churches. For they are not permitted to speak but should be subordinate, as the law also says" (1 Corinthians 14:34).

My dad was very patriarchal. He ruled the house, and whatever he said was the law. At times my mother, sister, and I lived in fear, for it felt that the women in the family existed to please and appease my father. He got away with his patriarchal thinking and actions using the church, God, and the Bible to back him up. My father's favorite verse for reminding my mother that she needed to be a good, obedient wife was, "Wives, be subject to your husbands as to the Lord, for the husband is the head of the wife just as Christ is the head of the church, his body, and is himself its Savior" (Ephesians 5:22-23). Every time he felt my mom was not listening or obeying him, he would recite these verses loudly to her to make sure she knew she was out of line and had to listen to him.

He often told me that men are closer to God since God is male. Therefore, God speaks to men and gives them messages to share with their wives and children. Since the message of God came through the father, it was essential that everyone listened and obeyed their father.

Since I lived in terror, I did not have the insight or opportunity to challenge his teachings. I just assumed that a white male God meant that those who looked white and were men were to have power over women, especially women of color. Being so naive about white patriarchal Christianity, I just accepted it as part of my faith, family, and church.

Men have enjoyed their privilege and their superiority over women for far too long. Both parties have accepted this supreme right, and thus far it has worked within the patriarchal Christian religion.

When we dig deep into our patriarchal world, we see how our religious beliefs, teachings, and doctrines are steeped in acts of violence. In Christian teachings, we lift up the stories of the Israelites invading and conquering other people as acts endorsed by God. We see Jesus being viewed as an innocent lamb, slaughtered, and sacrificed for our sins. These righteous acts of violence stem from our gendered understanding of God—a white male God who is almighty, powerful, and omniscient and does not tolerate disobedience.

A white masculine Christianity had to be implemented to maintain white men's power and authority in society and church.

When Americans speak of their long, proud tradition of democracy, they are speaking of a democracy that was only available to white folk. For Native people on the reservation, for African Americans in Jim Crow South, for Latinx folks throughout the Southwest, or the Japanese during the internment, this white-dominated society was devastating. The residue of this history is felt in white majority's entrenchment that continues to benefit white people today. Communities of color continue to follow laws and legislation that were enacted to protect and expand white supremacy.[7] Liberation is difficult for the disenfranchised as laws are not really there to protect us.

The white male God arose out of Greek philosophy, which upheld the dualism that has been so detrimental to Christianity. Divisions such as male and female, heaven and earth, spirit, and matter are used to make one better and preferable over the other and do not leave room for people of color, trans people, nonbinary people, and others who do not fall neatly into a dualistic world.

Since Christianity in North America has a big impact on all aspects of social and private life, it is impossible to ignore the correlation of constantly projecting a white male God and the violence committed against women and people of color. Christena Cleveland stresses the importance of imagination in theology: "We can only believe what we can imagine. And our cultural landscape hasn't given us many tools to imagine a non-white, non-male God."[8] Our churches have indoctrinated us to be followers of a white male God, and we have become blind and ignorant to the consequences of that. This powerful indoctrination has restrained and confined us from going outside the box to use our imaginations for reimagining God. We need to challenge ourselves and then reform and liberate Christianity so it will be life-giving to all people, not just white men.

FEMININE DIMENSION OF GOD

Patriarchy has tied women's identity to their husbands or fathers, and as such, their individuation has been stifled. Women have been twisted and altered, turned into villains in biblical contexts.

A white, Christian, patriarchal universe is a hospitable place for the dominant, aggressive, and often narcissistic white men.[9] For more than half the world's population, the world is a hostile place that legitimizes masculine aggression. Overcoming the pervasive error of the white male God means emphasizing the feminine dimension of God. God is described as a mother hen: "How often have I desired to gather your children together as a hen gathers her brood under her wings" (Matthew 23:37). In the Old Testament God is compared to a mother eagle: "As an eagle stirs up its nest and hovers over its young, as it spreads its wings, takes them up, and bears them aloft on its pinions" (Deuteronomy 32:11).

We should also note that one of the names for God, *El Shaddai*, can be understood to mean "God with Breasts." *El Shaddai* was known to be a fertility god—a god with breasts—and began in the early monarchy of Israel.[10] It was probably written by the Ephraimite authors during the time of Saul's reign (1025–1005 BCE). Breasts are most often associated with women, not men, so this points to a feminine dimension of the divine. There are other feminine references, for example Genesis 49:25: "By the God of your father, who will help you, by the Almighty who will bless you with blessings of heaven above, blessings of the deep that lies beneath, blessings of the breasts and of the womb."

Male traits such as aggressiveness and competitiveness that are thought to be innate are really manifestations of a patriarchal ideology that "sanctions the political and dominant role of men in the public and private spheres. By dominating the public sphere, men can control a culture's intellectual life. This then means that the male perspective becomes the standard source of knowledge and truth."[11] However, these characteristics only capture one limiting aspect of God.

We need to elevate the feminine divine who loves us and embraces us for who we are: women, people of color, broken and ambiguous. We need a God who destroys whiteness and patriarchy and invites us into her work of freedom, inclusion, and liberation. We desire a God who has a special place for and love of the marginalized, the outcast, and the broken-hearted because she is a God who has experienced these things and can heal them. We are in need of a God who destroys racism, xenophobia, discrimination, and domination, for such a God embraces us with all our imperfections, distinctions, vulnerabilities, and colorfulness.

Two biblical terms that can help us develop a feminine understanding of God are *Shekinah* and *Sophia*. Both of these are rooted in the biblical traditions that welcomed and embraced a feminine perception of the divine.

SHEKINAH

The Scriptures have liberative images and concepts of God that are helpful to women. For so long, many of these images became buried within church tradition and swept away under the rug in favor of emphasizing the masculine imagery of God who is powerful, almighty, and fearful, and who can wipe away the enemies like a powerful king. The people desired such a God as they dealt with invasion, colonialism, and exile. A God who can eliminate their enemies is the only God they wanted to worship. They projected their desires on God and used such words and categories to describe God. As a result, this only reinforced the patriarchy that was already present and continued to subordinate women.

However, there are feminine understandings and images of God that can help fight patriarchy. One such liberative model is the Old Testament image of Shekinah. Shekinah is a female figure of the divine presence who accompanied Israel into exile. This is a beautiful and comforting image that counters a theology of God's absence and God's patriarchal image, which has been destructive to women.[12] Shekinah as a feminine figure of the divine is a helpful and empowering image, especially for women. God as Shekinah is never away from God's people but is always with them and guiding them all throughout their path.

Shekinah is grammatically feminine and indicates the sense of being in a sacred place, drawn from the Hebrew root word *shakhan,* which means to be present or dwell as in a tabernacle, sanctuary, or tent (as in Exodus 25:8). Although the Shekinah has a relatively minor role in rabbinic Judaism, Shekinah in rabbinic literature is presented as the indwelling presence of God among the daily life of the Israelites. When Israel was unclean, the Shekinah was present with them, and even though evil drives her away, she watches over the sick. When a person is in pain, *Shekinah*'s head and arms also ache. The Shekinah's presence is in them as they suffer or experience brokenness. The Shekinah is a symbol of God's self-revelation and immanence in the everyday world.

In the earliest midrashim (biblical commentaries in narrative form) the Shekinah reveals God's presence with Israel, an exiled community, wherever they were or going. God's Shekinah was present in the exiled body of Israel, and the community of Israel was where God dwelled.[13] Thus the presence of God is not limited to a certain area but can be anywhere. This is the good news that we can embrace today. One cannot limit the presence of God, as God is present in all of God's creation and to all peoples. God will be where God will be. This is a comforting image of the presence of God. God wills to be with us in our differences and similarities; God's presence will be experienced by many.

Shekinah is a delightful and encouraging way to understand how God embraces all people despite our ethnicity, immigration status, or gender. Shekinah developed out of cultic language, and originally meant God's tabernacle, tent, and dwelling among God's people. It was first experienced in the transportable Ark, and then, after the entry into the temple, it was experienced on Zion. In the temple, the God of Israel finds rest and God is present in the sanctuary. The destruction of Jerusalem and the deportation of a section of the people into Babylonian exile raised the question about the presence of God among God's people. The *Shekinah* dwells among the worshiping community, in the synagogues, among the judges, with the wretched, with the sick, and so forth. The Shekinah shares Israel's joys and suffering and is present among the people. Moltmann notes,

> The Shekinah is not a divine attribute. It is the presence of God himself. But it is not God in his essential omnipresence. It is his special, willed, and promised presence in the world. The Shekinah is God himself, present at a particular place and at a particular time. . . . The Shekinah is certainly the present God, but this presence is distinguished from his eternity. If the Shekinah is the earthly, temporal and spatial presence of God, then it is at once identical with God and distinct from him. Because of this, later rabbinic and kabbalistic scholars tried to think of the Shekinah as a hypostasis, an intermediary or go-between, or a divine emanation.[14]

Some rabbinic commentators thought that the destruction of the temple was a sign of the Shekinah's desertion of the Jewish people on account of their sins. But God is compassionate and loving; the Shekinah is always present and shares in Israel's suffering in exile. In the absence of the temple, the home is the place of her presence. The symbolics of the (remembered) home do not prevent the conditions for God's presence in Auschwitz. Women deported out of the holy could fulfill God's command to make God a sanctuary so that God could live among them (Exodus 25:8) because God, as Shekinah, is a wandering God, and Jewish sacred space is mobile. In the early biblical period sacred space was established wherever Jews were encamped in the barren wilderness around them. From the rabbinic period to the present, God's presence is not limited to a specific place but is marked by God's people, Israel, who carry God's presence with them.[15] God is Spirit and cannot be limited or bound by space or time. God can be anywhere and everywhere. God as Shekinah provides us comfort as we move, knowing that God cannot be bound and limited to one location.

The subordination of women and the repression of the feminine divine occurred through much of history. Male traits such as aggressiveness and competitiveness that are thought to be inborn are rather manifestations of patriarchy that allows the dominant role of men in the public, in faith communities, and in private spheres. By dominating the public sphere, men take control of culture and society. This means that the male perspective becomes the standard source of knowledge and truth,[16] and women's views and understandings are not sought or regarded.

The Shekinah is frequently viewed as a shining light, and she is understood as an image of the female aspect of God who cares deeply for her people in exile. The writers of the rabbinic period regarded the Shekinah as a personification of God beyond just a literary device: God's closeness to the suffering Israel and her sharing in Israel's exile was central to the maintenance of faith.

The Israelites wanted to avoid falling into ditheism and thus the rabbis would not hypostasize her as a divine being.[17] In a patriarchal culture where men read and interpret Scripture, the feminine presence of God was often pushed to the margins. This is how patriarchy is reinforced. However, with new interpretations and understandings of the Shekinah, we can begin to see it as a life-giving and important liberative image for women.

Shekinah is a liberative figure—a divine feminine presence that accompanied Israel into exile. This is a powerful and comforting image that counters a theology of a God removed and inaccessible except through male priests and church leaders. God as Shekinah is never away from God's people but is always with them, guiding them throughout their path. Thus, the presence of God is not limited to a certain area but can be anywhere. This is the good news that we all carry with us. One cannot limit the presence of God; God is present in all of God's creation.

SOPHIA

The church has been focused on masculine terms and names for God, but Scripture also includes feminine words for God such as *Hokmah* (wisdom in Hebrew) and *Sophia* (wisdom in Greek). Wisdom is feminine in both languages. This makes a difference in how we view God and understand ourselves. These feminine words need to be emphasized and used in the church so we can have a holistic understanding of God, not just a masculine concept. They should be incorporated into our languages, liturgies, prayers, hymns, and sermons so it makes us rethink our long history of patriarchal languages.

In my first book, *The Grace of Sophia*,[18] I discuss the feminine dimension of God understood as wisdom. Sophia is present in the Old Testament and in the New Testament and is understood as the feminine presence of God. In both Hebrew and Greek, the words are feminine and emphasize the feminine dimension of God. This feminine dimension of God is biblical, historical, and Christian, but it has been pushed under the rug and ignored by many.

Sophia is present in various places in the Old Testament. She is found in Proverbs 8:22-31, where she was with God before creation and was a co-creator with God.

> The LORD created me at the beginning of his work,
>> the first of his acts of long ago.
> Ages ago I was set up,
>> at the first, before the beginning of the earth.
> When there were no depths, I was brought forth,
>> when there were no springs abounding with water.
> Before the mountains had been shaped,
>> before the hills, I was brought forth,
> when he had not yet made earth and fields,
>> or the world's first bits of soil.
> When he established the heavens, I was there,
>> when he drew a circle on the face of the deep,
> when he made firm the skies above,
>> when he established the fountains of the deep,
> when he assigned to the sea its limit,
>> so that the waters might not transgress his command,
> when he marked out the foundations of the earth,
>> then I was beside him, like a master worker;
> and I was daily his delight,
>> playing before him always,
> playing in his inhabited world
>> and delighting in the human race. (Proverbs 8:22-31)

This passage illustrates how Sophia was with God rejoicing in the creation of the world and of humanity. The feminine dimension of God is present in Sophia. Some would even argue that if Jesus is the son of God, then Sophia is the daughter of God who delights in being in the presence of God and co-creating with God.

There are also passages about Lady Wisdom in the streets as found in Proverbs 1:20-33, where it begins, "Wisdom cries out in the street; in the squares as she raises her voice. At the busiest corner she cries out; at the entrance of the city gates she speaks" (Proverbs 1:20-21). Wisdom is portrayed as a feminine prophet. Just as the male prophets Isaiah, Jeremiah, and Ezekiel before her, she cries out to the people, and when they do not listen, she will not answer to them when they call out later. She warns that destruction will come to the fools but goodness to those who listen to her. She runs through the streets like a preacher who makes a strong appeal to whomever will listen to her pleas. Lady Wisdom is calling people to seek wisdom and to seek God. Wisdom is the presence of the word of God in the world.

Sophia, the feminine imagery of God who is found both in the Old Testament, the New Testament, and in the early church, slowly starts to disappear and is filled in by the masculine *logos*. The attributes of wisdom become transferred onto Jesus. We see Jesus crying out in the streets, preparing a table, and giving life to those who seek just as Wisdom has done in the Old Testament times.

Wisdom is viewed as the tree of life and the source of nourishment who is offering her fruit to those who hunger and thirst.[19] All these Judaic attributes of Wisdom are then assigned to Jesus in the birth of Christianity. Just like Wisdom, Jesus is portrayed as the source of nourishment, the tree of life, and the one we turn to if we hunger and thirst. Jesus becomes the Wisdom that is found in the Old Testament. Jesus becomes the God incarnate and is the image of the invisible God (Colossians 1:15).

In Scripture, the feminine Wisdom is clearly associated with God and assigned to Jesus. "In contrast, God is why you are in Christ Jesus, who became for us wisdom from God, and righteousness and sanctification and redemption" (1 Corinthians 1:30). Jesus is Wisdom and therefore embodies a feminine dimension of God. This is provocative news that got sidelined by male leaders.

There are other New Testament passages that link Jesus to the wisdom of God. "The Son of Man came eating and drinking, and they say, 'Look, a glutton and a drunkard, a friend of tax collectors and sinners!' Yet wisdom is vindicated by her deeds" (Matthew 11:19). Here again we see that Jesus is wisdom which implies that Jesus as God is also feminine. However, the patriarchal context and religion eliminated this feminine dimension of God, and the focus is only on *logos* and the maleness of Jesus.

John's prologue reads, "In the beginning was the Word, and the Word was with God, and the Word was God" (John 1:1). But scholars "detect an association with Jewish wisdom (Sophia)" underneath the language of Word/*logos*.[20] If this is the case, the text would be better understood as "In the beginning was the Wisdom and the Wisdom was with God, and the Wisdom was God" (John 1:1). This is in line with Proverbs 8:22-31, where Wisdom is co-creating with God: "Ages ago I was set up, at the first, before the beginning of the earth . . . then I was beside him, like a master worker" (Proverbs 8:23, 30). "Wisdom is depicted as a person accompanying God in the act of creation. The Word's personification and creative activity in John's prologue suggests a link with Jewish *Sophia*. . . . John's personification of the Word draws on the personification of Sophia."[21] This emphatically shows that Sophia is God, which then reinforces the feminine divine.

If wisdom is the original understanding, then the rejection of it makes clear the patriarchal tendencies of the church. In certain ways, John's prologue presents a prologue to the incarnation of Jesus as the story of Sophia. Sophia participates and is active in the creation of the world. She comes down from heaven and pitches a tent among God's people. Sophia is rejected by humanity but offers life to those who seek and becomes a big light in the world that cannot be overcome by darkness (John 1:1-18).[22]

Jesus who is understood as wisdom incarnate is found in different places in the New Testament. Paul in 1 Corinthians confirms that Jesus is "the wisdom of God" (1 Corinthians 1:24), and John's prologue also connects Jesus as the wisdom of God and as God. This belief and understanding in the New Testament that Christ as God is articulated as wisdom shows a shift from the Old Testament sapientology (theology of wisdom). Sapientology is the understanding that the divine wisdom is not really God but an attribute of God. This shift is significant and occurred about twenty years after the death of Jesus. This was a time when source material for much of the New Testament was being gathered and written. Therefore the possibility of the shift in this understanding of wisdom was intentional and not accidental. The probability is that wisdom sayings in the New Testament are a way of identifying Jesus as God's wisdom. Wisdom was not just a trait of God but was God.[23] *Logos* carried much of the meaning of Sophia and *Hokmah* into the New Testament times. Thus, even if "word" is not equivalent to "wisdom," John as a Jewish Christian infused his understanding of logos with the Hebrew understanding of Sophia in his writings.

In New Testament times, there were some negative attitudes toward feminine concepts like Wisdom. Then, Philo, who believed strongly in gender dualism, linked Wisdom to logos and identified anything feminine as "transient, imperfect, physical, earthly, irrational, passive and even evil."[24] As Christianity became so heavily influenced by dualism, the church opted to embrace *logos,* the word of God, over Sophia, the wisdom of God. Many believed that Jesus is the *logos,* and thus it was much easier to accept the masculine incarnation of God rather than embrace a feminine image of God. This acceptance of *logos* only perpetuated the maleness of God, which then influenced the patriarchy of Christianity.

Logos continues to prevail today and is prevalent in our churches, theology, and faith seeking understanding. The preference for maleness in our understanding of God and Jesus speaks volumes to our preconceived notions of the divine. Men have projected themselves on God and with their power have maintained it regardless of scriptural and traditional references to a feminine identification of God. The present white church has held onto the masculine identity of Jesus and has embraced Jesus as the *logos*—masculine—and rejected Jesus as Sophia, the feminine.

Christianity today would be different if we focused on Sophia rather than *logos.* This feminine understanding of God turns our understanding of God upside down. It goes against all the one-sided masculine, authoritative, fearful images of God and presents a God who takes care, loves, and rejoices in us. Sophia presents a hopeful reimagining of God in a patriarchal world. It saves women.

Words and images are powerful and form our thoughts, beliefs, and actions. Words form our concepts of Jesus and who he is. All these words for Jesus and God are mere symbols, metaphors and analogies for God. We cannot fathom the fullness of God, and we only have words, images, concepts to help us understand the God and Jesus whom we encounter. Those in power have chosen a white male Jesus over the feminine Sophia who is nonracialized. This has cemented a white male God for most of Christian history.

When I began to research Sophia, many of my conservative friends thought I was doing useless work on something that was "evil" and not even Christian. Many of my Korean evangelical friends thought that my starting a PhD in theology would sway me away from the hardcore truth of Christianity. But the reality was that my Korean evangelical Christian friends were afraid I would challenge the white male God and white masculine Christianity they had come to accept and love. They embraced the false belief that a white God saved Korea from economic ruin and placed the nation at the forefront of innovation, cultural growth, and economic prosperity. Any message that might contradict that would shake the foundation of their faith.

Many men want to keep the white male God and uphold him as a ticket to success, power, and domination. Many of my Korean evangelical friends thought I was on a road to atheism and becoming a heathen for endeavoring a nonwhite and nonmale understanding of God. But if we are to gain peace and any form of liberation for women and people of color, we must eliminate the white male God.

Catholics do not ordain women, but an international movement called Roman Catholic Women Priests ordains women as priests in the Catholic Church. Their mission is to prepare and ordain in apostolic succession women who are called by the Holy Spirit to priestly ministry.[25] This growing group looks to the feminine dimension of God who empowers them to become priests to lead, teach, preach, and serve sacraments in the church. One of my former students is part of this group and recently got ordained into the Catholic Church. The Roman Catholic Church does not recognize this group, but a growing number of people are seeing the need for these women priests.

In Korea, where it is difficult for many women to seek ordination in the church, "women churches" have formed where they ordain women as ministers of the church and most of the congregation members are women. These suffering and oppressed women seek liberation within this large group of women leaders and ministers. They have sought the feminine wisdom of God as a solace to their patriarchal oppression in society and the church. I hope biblical images like the Shekinah and Sophia will continue to be meaningful, uplifting, and empowering many of us in search of the feminine divine. This will ultimately save women.

9

LIBERATING WHITENESS

In my conservative evangelical Christian upbringing, it was considered evil and wrong to reimagine God. Even questioning the God taught to us would move us toward a loving, embracing, and holy God, but venturing outside of the white male God was considered unacceptable, syncretistic, and inconceivable. It was the stuff of heresy, and I would have been asked to leave the church.

If God is not white and male, then who is God? God does not embrace patriarchy but actually diminishes it and disrupts power to empower us all to join in God's liberating work. God is a God of compassion who seeks to liberate all enslaved, marginalized, and oppressed peoples. God healed the lepers who were outcasts and not part of society. God engaged with the Samaritan woman at the well who was shunned by the Jews. God heard the plea of the Syrophoenician woman who begged Jesus to heal her daughter.

God is a God of love, grace, and mercy who cherishes our humanity and welcomes our fears, vulnerabilities, and imperfections.[1] God is not the angry white male God that Christianity has given us for the past two thousand years. God is a disruptor of the status quo. God isn't the powerful white king God who wants to cast aside sinners and lift up white men as leaders. God does the opposite and stands with those at the margins.

To work toward a just society, we must make a paradigm shift where we recognize that there is a plurality of centers and embrace that rather than searching for purity. We embrace hybridity, difference, and liberty instead.

In order to liberate ourselves from whiteness, white supremacy, and racism, we must extricate whiteness, white nationalism, and discrimination from Christianity and from the church. Liberative Christianity is a progressive, reforming, and subversive way of understanding Christianity that attempts to get to the true Jesus rather than the traditionally white, imperialistic Jesus that has dominated Christianity for the past two thousand years. Christianity needs to unpack and unlearn what we have been taught and decolonize societies, Christianity, and churches from white male domination. Speaking truth to power leads us to different ways of thinking and practice that might bring about radical change.

Jesus spoke from the margins, and Christianity emerged as a religion for the poor, the disenfranchised, and the marginalized, not for the rich white male colonizing powers. Over time Christianity became widely organized into a bureaucratic religion headlined by rulers, kings, and corrupt churchmen, moving away from the message of compassion, love, and charity that Jesus taught. We must study and understand the social constraints and problems that confine so many to poverty and how racism has marginalized people of color.

When Christianity is co-opted by the rulers, it becomes a dominating device rather than a gathering of unified followers where all are equal and cherished, where everyone works together to bring harmony to a divided world.

LIBERATING THE WHITE MALE GOD

God is a personal God who is with us and within us. But the traditional whiteness and maleness of God has invaded our thoughts and minds and how we understand and relate to God. It is in our churches, schools, communities, and homes as it has been passed on through tradition, hymns, liturgies, and prayers. This whiteness and maleness of God is unrelatable to the majority of people in the world. But this is the God who has been perpetuated all throughout Christianity and is even embedded in our culture and society. It has no liberative force. We need to loosen our grip on this whiteness and maleness of God that has been destructive, deadly, divisive, problematic, and damaging.

The time has come for reckoning with whiteness and the white male God. The time to reimagine God is long overdue. We must reimagine God as a loving and embracing God who loves all of humanity and not just the ones a small group deems acceptable.

When communities of color present God as Black, Christians get alarmed that it is heretical. James Cone wrote about a Black God from his work out of his cultural and racial identity and history. This really helps not only the African American community but all of us get to a deeper understanding of God and God's work and presence in our world. Cone explores the similarity and difference between the cross and the lynching tree, which are both symbols of death; the cross, however, symbolizes hope and salvation while the lynching tree signifies the negation of the message by white supremacy.[2]

Lynching of Black America as mob violence and torture directed against Blacks began to increase after the civil war and end of slavery. This was tied to the 1867 Congress decision to pass the Reconstruction Act, granting Black men the franchise and citizenship rights of participation in the affairs of government. The

Ku Klux Klan, organized as a social club in Pulaski, Tennessee (1866), transformed into a vigilante group whose purpose was to save the South and ensure that America remained a white person's country. They couldn't allow Blacks to ever rule over whites. White supremacists felt insulted by the suggestion that whites and Blacks might work together as equals.[3] As lynchings and racial attacks increased and Black oppression continued, the need grew to reexamine who God is and whether God will allow such horrendous acts of evil to continue. A white God reinforces white supremacy, and therefore theological reimagination is required to understand that God is on the side of the oppressed, the enslaved, the lynched, and the broken. If this is true, then God must be Black. God's Blackness means that God has made the oppressed condition of Blacks into God's own condition and priority. God cares about the context and situation that people find themselves in, and God liberates and frees the oppressed and the enslaved. We saw this when God took the Israelites in Egypt out of enslavement. Therefore, it is important to listen to voices other than the white-dominant voice to gain a deeper and more liberative understanding of the gospel message and of who God is.

When Asian Americans bring in Asian concepts to help expand our understanding of God, people begin to shout syncretism and claim it is not real Christianity. White people pretend that white Eurocentric male Christians never syncretized their beliefs, practices, and traditions. Many white people actually believe that their Christianity is pure, authentic, and the only true form of Christianity divinely given to white people for all of humanity. They want to share this belief to all peoples around the globe. However, we must acknowledge that Christianity is not pristine but tainted by cultural, contextual, and historical influences. This is true not just of people of color's understanding of Christianity but also of white people's version of Christianity. It is good to have multiple readings of theology and Christianity, as it helps widen our perspective and understandings of God. Every people, nation, and social location has something to contribute to a fuller, deeper, more meaningful picture and comprehension of God.

Christianity has always been a mixing of various cultures and religious practices. For example, if we look at Anselm's theory of atonement, he used European cultural concepts and ideas such as lord and serf from his own period in the Middle Ages. Additionally, when we come together to celebrate Easter, we must not ignore its pagan roots and practices. The inclusion of Easter eggs is a pagan practice that has become a staple image during Easter. Easter started out as a celebration of the spring equinox, a time when all of nature awakens from winter and the cycle of renewal begins anew. Anglo-Saxon pagans celebrated this rebirth by invoking *Eostre* or *Ostara*, the goddess of spring and fertility. Pagans decorated eggs to celebrate rebirth and gift them to family and friends. This does not have anything to do with the resurrection of Jesus Christ from the tomb. But it all eventually became part of white Christian Easter celebrations, which is an example of syncretism. When white Christians engage in syncretism it is never understood to be syncretism. Rather it is simply accepted as Christianity and Christian tradition. It is only when people of color engage in syncretism that people get alarmed and nervous about it.

We know that God is Spirit, but we have given God human characteristics. We also need to move away from an anthropomorphic Christianity centered on human beings and become more God-centered. The anthropomorphizing of God turned God into a white male God. This white male God became so entrenched into Christianity, theology, and doctrines that no one dared to question it or challenge it until more recent times. Marginalized and oppressed peoples are now challenging this white male God imagery as we know it was used to legitimize our subordination and subjugation. If we do not contest it, the coercion toward marginalized groups will continue in the name of Christianity.

God is beyond our own words and imaginations. Our finite human minds cannot conceive an infinite God. God is that which we cannot fully comprehend and understand. God cannot be bound by the limitations and imaginations of human beings. Exodus 3:14 states, "I AM WHO I AM." We cannot limit God's eternity and how "God will be who God will be." We cannot confine God to our little minds, as God is beyond ourselves. Augustine said, "If we think that is God, that is not God."

We have all been created in the image of God. Genesis 1:27 states, "So God created humans in his image, in the image of God he created them, male and female he created them." We all—women, Black, Asians, Africans, straight, LGBTQ+, abled, disabled, educated, noneducated, rich, and poor—are included in the image of God, not just the white European men.

The oppressive male white image of God needs to be liberated and freed. When this happens we will view God through the lens of not only white people but also Black, Asian American, Native American, Hispanic, and invisible people around the globe. People can bring their different languages, concepts, words, and experiences to widen and expand our limited understanding of God. Only if we do this will the oppressive male white image of God be freed. As a result, this will free white Christians and white Christianity from their own whiteness. Whiteness and white supremacy continue to go against the work and message of God. God is with the oppressed and loves the stranger, foreigner, refugee, and immigrant. Liberating white people from the message of whiteness will free them to work for the oppressed and live out the gospel message. As a result, this will help white people to do the work of God and free Christianity to build the kin-dom of God that embraces all people and work toward equity and liberation. White people are then liberated to become more fully human when they see a larger picture of God and Christianity beyond their own whiteness. Further, we can all worship and embrace a God who first loved us and who continues to show mercy, grace, and hope— this is the God of Christianity who has been lost and buried under white supremacy. We need to challenge this if we are to get to the core of God's love and everlasting hope.

Our spiritual imaginations need to venture beyond the Protestant white male God. Patriarchy does not want us to have the adventurous spiritual audacity to ask boundary-pushing questions about God and establish connection to our true, uncontrollable power. In order to encounter the divine truth that lies beyond what we think we know, we have to excavate our cultural landscape to uncover the hidden work of this white male God and forge a new path.

God, the author of diversity, is the unifying presence within diversity. If we can only see beyond with our hearts to the other, we will not be enemies. We will learn to love those who are different from us. We will even rejoice in our differences and welcome diversity in our lives. We need to see in each other a trace of the divine Other.[4] Quakers have a phrase, "That of God in everyone." If we can truly believe this and accept this in our lives, it will be a life-changing way of being in this world. Recognizing the divine in each other will prevent wars, genocide, patriarchy, racism, and domination.

Tolerance comes not from the absence of conviction but from its living presence. Understanding the particularity of what matters to us is the best way of coming to appreciate what matters to others. Difference does not diminish; it enlarges the sphere of human possibilities. We will learn to live with diversity once we understand the God-given, world-enhancing dignity of difference.[5] This will make this world a happier, loving, and peaceful place. Without further hesitation, we must begin the work of liberating our white male God for the sake of all humanity.

A THEOLOGY OF VISIBILITY

I have written about a theology of visibility in my book *Invisible*[6] to articulate a way to help the marginalized become more visible in society. It is also a theology that makes the invisible God visible to those who have been made invisible and marginalized by the white-dominant society. A theology of visibility turns us toward a path where we don't forget about the racialized, stereotyped, subordinated, and discriminated individuals in our society. To overcome some of the pain of being made invisible by the white-dominant society, I propose a theology of visibility that will help us overcome the darkest pains of racism, discrimination, and xenophobia and work toward a God who embraces us all.

A theology of visibility uses four Korean terms, *han, ou-ri, jeong*, and *Chi*, which are helpful in dismantling a white male God and working toward a liberative and loving God. *Han* is a Korean term meaning "unjust suffering" and tries to capture the pain and suffering one endures due to unjust systems such as racism, sexism, and classism. *Ou-ri* means "us" and is a significant term in Asian culture as Asians emphasize the "us" and not the "I" like the Western world. *Ou-ri* takes us away from individualism and orients us toward a communal understanding of the kin-dom of God that includes all people. This is a critical concept to reorient ourselves to the importance of community. If we recognize that community is essential, then we will begin our work to accept and honor everyone in our community, no matter how different they are from us. The community is what keeps us, feeds us, and protects us. We need to accept the theological key aspect of *ou-ri* in our faith journey toward a liberating God.

Jeong is a Korean word for love, reminding us how love is sticky and unbreakable. A loving relationship doesn't end due to a fight but endures as *jeong* keeps the relationship going. It is like the passage in Romans, "Neither death, nor life, nor angels, nor rulers . . . will be able to separate us from the love of God" (Romans 8:38). *Jeong* keeps the *ou-ri* alive in our journey of faith as we recognize our connectedness to each other and to the community. The *jeong* between each other will cement the necessity of being in relationship with others for our own flourishing, survival, and happiness.

Chi is an Asian term for spirit and is a helpful concept for us living in the West as it assists us to overcome the dualistic tendencies of white Christianity. White Christianity views the body as evil as well as matter, but in Eastern philosophy, the body is important. *Chi* seeks bodies, for it is within our bodies that we experience the dynamic flow of *Chi*, and it is *Chi* that heals us physically and spiritually. We must allow the free movement of *Chi* to strengthen us, heal us, motivate us to do the work of God.

In terms of etymology, *Chi* bears the closest resemblance to "spirit." The original meaning was "mist" or the vapor rising from a sacrificial offering. Spirit comes from the Latin *spiritus*, meaning "breath." English words with the same root that still refer explicitly to breath, and the analogous words in Hebrew, classical Greek, and Sanskrit (*ruakh, pneuma,* and *prana*) similarly cover the range of meanings from wind and breath to spirit. Some modern colloquial usages of Chi are similar to "high spirits."[7]

The vital material force *Chi* of the universe is that which joins humans and nature, unifying their worldview and ethos and giving humans the potential to become co-creators with the universe. It is *Chi* that unites rightness (ethos) and the Way (worldview), filling the whole space between heaven and earth.[8]

Chi flows in the body, and where the mind goes the *Chi* follows. By imaging and willing *Chi* to a certain area of the body, say a damaged part, it is believed that healing energy will surround that area. Indeed, mind is a correlative of the body, and the Chinese do not restrict this to the brain. *Chi* is understood to encompass both mind and body. The Chinese worldview sees a person with a vigorous body with strong *Chi* and a healthy mind with flowing emotions displaying energetic *Chi*.[9] Without *Chi*, we cannot work for any justice. When we die, our bodies get cold as *Chi* leaves our body and it is *Chi* that keeps us alive and warm. We cannot live without *Chi*. *Chi* is invisible and unseen. But as it is within our bodies, it allows and helps us to become more visible. It is the energy, power, vibration that works within our bodies, minds, and selves and that helps us to become visible as children of God in a society which wants to make us invisible.

This theology of visibility is helpful as we come to see the invisible God through the faces of those who have been made invisible in society. When we see that the invisible people of society are all beautifully created by God, we then come to see that God is not male or white. This is when we can come to embrace a God who is Spirit.

SPIRIT GOD

A liberative way of understanding God is to view God as Spirit. Spirit is genderless and raceless. Focusing on the Spirit of God can help us move past some of the dualistic problems within

Christianity, which led Christians to choose *logos* over Sophia and has had many consequential results which are detrimental to women and people of color. Being open to other words for Spirit, such as the Asian concept of *Chi*, helps us recognize the presence of the Spirit of God around the globe. Many cultures and religions have understood the importance of the Spirit—what we Christians have known as the Holy Spirit—to affect human lives for thousands of years before European missionaries ever stepped foot on the continent.

Spirit can be a doorway to open dialogue among people of all cultures and religions. The Spirit helps us move beyond difference and find common ground when we talk about the divine, ensuring that all people are welcomed to the table and engaged in the social justice issues of our time. Spirit God is biblical and is present in the Hebrew Bible as well as the New Testament. It is what motivates us to work for God and do what is good. When Christian theologians talk about the Holy Spirit, they always mean God, never merely one of God's gifts. The Spirit is the giver of life.

When I started teaching, my church historian friend said, "You theologians just make everything up. We church historians use historical church documents, biblical scholars use Scripture, but you theologians use 'nothing' and just make things up." I laughed but then assured him that we theologians don't make things up. We use Scripture, church history documents, and other creeds, traditions, and historical theology to inform our theology. Spirit God *is* biblical, and it has long been part of the church tradition. It is in our creeds and the doctrine of the Trinity. We are just evolving our understanding of the role and characteristics of Spirit. Theology uses other disciplines to help us understand God. The more means, tools, and languages we have, the deeper we can go to meet God. We can never know the fullness of God, as God is infinite and we are finite beings. We need to understand our limitations. But this does not prevent us from trying to find and understand who God is. It doesn't preclude us from searching for understanding and knowing God.

In my search for the God who is not white or gendered, the only biblical term and concept that made sense is the Spirit God. Spirit God is beyond gender, race, and ethnicity. Spirit God becomes the ultimate reality toward which we can set our eyes, while not knowing the fullness of God. Spirit God is the being of God that sets God free to be who God is and simultaneously sets us free too.

We must strive for liberative ways to approach, read, and interpret Scripture if we are to combat patriarchy, the maleness of God, and the subordination of women. Spirit language corrects some of these problems. The concept of the Spirit of God moves us away from the masculine language about God impacting our theological perception of God, expanding it to a more inclusive understanding of God. This movement away from the maleness of God will have significant impact on how the church and society views, understands, and treats women and trans people.

Spirit God is always within us. It is what has given us life and sustains us throughout our life. We are the holy temples of God, and this knowledge should make all the difference in how we treat ourselves, others, and nature. As we live in this ever-growing society of multi-national corporations, imperialism, and colonialism, we need to take a deep breath and recognize these dangers and work toward justice and peace. This is ever crucial to us as we try to live on this planet and to save it for the next generations.

Examining the history of race and the birth of whiteness becomes a strategic starting point to understanding our present political, social, and religious context. The creation of white identity shows insight into why it was so important to continue importing enslaved Africans to work in the plantations and how it was deemed acceptable to treat them harshly and inhumanely. This racialization of white people as well as people of color continued to satisfy the power of white people.

We need to move away from a raced and gendered God. A masculine white God has perpetuated sexism and racism deep within church and society. To achieve any form of justice and peace, we need to seek ways of reimagining and talking about a nonwhite and nongendered God. One way is to talk about the Shekinah and Sophia and emphasize the feminine dimension of God. This will do wonders to half the world's population who feel suppressed, subordinated, and subjugated by the church's teachings of patriarchy which was reinforced by a white male God. Another way is to use Spirit language.

The God of visibility makes the marginalized visible and uplifts them. Spirit God is nongendered, nonracialized, nonwhite, and nonbinary. Spirit God is the life-giving God who embraces and cherishes all of us regardless of how we look, walk, love, dress, or eat. Spirit God loves us just the way we are, without any consideration of our zip code, education, gender identity, sexual orientation, and ability. Spirit God is present in our midst as Spirit-Chi, who is liberative and embracing. Spirit God reaches out and finds us in our brokenness, gives us life, lives in us, and embraces us in spite of our downfalls and shortcomings. This is the embracing Spirit God of *Chi* and *jeong* who loves us with everything. Spirit God sustains us in this chaotic world of racism, sexism, whiteness, and prejudices. Spirit God will turn us away from racism and move toward love, wholeness, and *jeong*.

We must work to dismantle the white male God every day as it makes its way into politics, schools, churches, and neighborhoods until it is eradicated. We need to continue to reimagine Spirit God in liberative ways, such as the feminine divine and use this image to move away from a destructive white male. Feminine divine provides inspiration and possibilities to women around the globe. It reveals that they are also living in the image of the divine who inspires us to work for the good of everyone. It reminds us that we are to love our neighbors, feed the poor, and liberate the oppressed.

The feminine divine and Spirit God helps us reimagine new and better realities and revision a more just world of equality and equity among genders, racialized peoples, and those who are different from a white male normative center. Spirit God empowers us to embrace those who are marginalized and oppressed, and to engage in the work to build the kin-dom of God. We cannot do this on our own, but only with the help of Spirit God who vibrates, energizes, and strengthens us to do the work of God.

Spirit God who is loving and embracing cannot be destructive at the same time. Therefore, it is life-giving that we turn to Spirit God to move toward a loving, kind, welcoming, embracing, and graceful Spirit God.

10

EMBRACING A NONWHITE AND NONGENDERED GOD

Throughout this book we have considered the whiteness of how Christianity was shaped and how it continues to influence individuals and society. Through this influence, whiteness has infiltrated much of North American culture, economics, and politics, as well as religion. For Christians, whiteness has caused great damage in reinforcing the notion of a white male God, teaching that white men are at the top of the social ladder and people of color, especially woman of color, are at the bottom of the hierarchy.

My goal is to work toward reimagining a nonwhite and a nongendered God—a God who can help us build a more just society, faith community, and loving church. Spirit God will teach us that everyone is equal and everyone, regardless of gender, race, and ethnicity, is welcomed into the body of Christ. But how do we incorporate these new practices into our lives so we can move toward a nonwhite and nongendered God who embraces all people? We reimagine God by rethinking and rewriting worship and liturgy, reconsidering discipleship, and reshaping our community of faith. Reconceptualizing our understanding of God will inform and impact our behavior in church and society.

WORSHIP AND LITURGY

For most of the church's history, our prayers, hymns, and liturgies have been written by white European men. The language used in our church worship imagines, describes, and reinforces a white male God. From the beginning to the end of worship, we praise, read about, and pray to a white male God. This is consistent through many denominations as they cling to their hymnals, prayer books, and other worship guides.

The white male language used throughout our religious practice reinforces our perceptions and beliefs that white and male is superior to nonwhite and female. We memorize prayers, hymns, and creeds during childhood that become embedded in our thoughts, hearts, and behaviors that end up carried into adulthood. These white male liturgies have become part of our being and greatly influence our perception of God.

Moving away from this white male God through our liturgy is an important step in guiding us toward a more just society where one race is not intrinsically elevated. Instead, we learn that everyone is equal and beautifully created by God and God does not have a racial or gendered identity.

In the church, we use language in our attempts to define and understand God. Words equip us with a way to express our understanding of each other, the world, and God. Continuing to use non-inclusive liturgical language of God—Lord, Father, Almighty, Sovereign—only reinforces the notion that God is white and male. We know that God is neither white nor male. That was merely a notion of God constructed by white male theologians. God is Spirit and, as a spiritual entity, cannot have gender or race, and this should be reflected in the liturgical languages that we use within the church.

It is paramount that we rethink and re-create our liturgical language about God. One way we can do this is to shift our focus from using titles to describe God, such as Father, Lord, and Sovereign, to using words that convey action in the way we refer to God in our liturgies. There are inclusive hymnals and liturgical books, such as *Inclusive Hymns for Liberating Christians*[1] that move away from a patriarchal understanding of God. For ministers and preachers, there is Wil Gafney's *A Women's Lectionary for the Whole Church*,[2] which introduces unexamined perspectives of biblical translation of Scripture that are helpful for sermon and Bible study preparations. These new emerging liturgical resources help widen our perspectives and encourage us to consciously make inclusive choices in worship, preaching, teaching, adult forums, and Sunday school.

In Scripture, the Spirit of God is portrayed as breath, wind, light, and vibration, which are in many ways actions of the Spirit. The Spirit moves and dwells among us and in us. The Spirit is active, flowing, and changing spaces for us. These words reveal to us how God moves in the world and even within us. We breathe in air, and the wind blows wherever it wishes; the light shines on us, and we can feel vibrations in us and around us. This is God being present in us and in our lives. These are action or movement words to talk about the Spirit of God in the world and in our presence. These are beautiful ways to reimagine and think about God because they not only remove the white maleness that is so problematic, but they also are far more accurate and meaningful ways to conceptualize and connect with God. There is power, love, grace, and peace in these movement words. Ultimately, God is a God who acts within our lives and in the world. God hears our prayers and comes to us through the movement of the Spirit to comfort us, heal us, and renew us. Reframing God as Spirit in motion, acting in our best interests and filling us with the love, guidance, and sustenance we need, brings us in closer communion and relationship with God.

One of the best places to start is thinking of God as Breath. When human beings were created, God breathed into them to give them life. This action is the origin of everything we are, and it comes from a loving God.

Another example of how we can revise our language is to change our prayers this way: "Loving God of Light, who lights up the world and guides us during times of turmoil and difficulties. We thank you for your grace." God as light sheds brightness into our dark spaces, and the power of light to remove darkness is helpful for those of us struggling to survive in this world that can feel bleak and hopeless. This is a brilliant and life-giving shift from the patriarchal and white God that is conveyed through traditional liturgy.

We can view God as the wind moving barriers in our way. It was the Spirit of God as wind that parted the Red Sea so the Israelites could flee the Egyptians who were after them. Wind spreads the seeds for new life to form. Birds ride the wind to carry them to greater heights and farther distances. Wind creates power. Considering God in these terms helps us see a force that is moving in and through us, raising us up, carrying us over obstacles to plant us where we can flourish.

We can also speak of God as vibration. When God said, "Let there be light," it was the vibration of God's words into the world that created light out of darkness. There is influence and impact in vibrations as they create, heal, empower, and love. Vibration is the unseen movement of energy. It can manifest as a feeling/sensation or a sound, and it can be felt in the deepest parts of us. God as vibration tells us that we are filled by the Spirit as God moves within us and among us, empowering us to take the light and love God created into the world.

In Exodus 3:14 God says to Moses, "I AM WHO I AM. . . . Thus you shall say to the Israelites: 'I AM has sent me to you.'" This name of God is a form of the verb "to be." Hence, God Spirit as wind, light, breath, and vibration are in line with the understanding of God's name as action. This emphasizes the mystery of God and encourages us to continuously explore and reimagine God who is greater than anything we can ever imagine.

Our acts of worship should be intentional and welcoming for everyone who enters God's sanctuary. We must acknowledge our limitations and welcome new liturgical language about God to liberate and empower us and not limit our understanding of God. We pray at home and in our churches, and our prayers need to lead to some action that will help us see the God who is loving and embracing to all and not just to certain groups of people. Our prayers cannot just be thoughts; they must lead to some provocative change and action in our world.

COMMUNITY

Community building and communal existence are essential for overcoming racial and gender injustices. The West has become more and more focused on individual desires than community needs, which has led to prejudices and biases. When the "I" comes before the "we," what the individual wants becomes of utmost importance, often at the expense of what is best for the group as a whole. This self-prioritization fosters a sense of vulnerability, and the other is viewed as a threat to the well-being and safety of the individual.

The "isms" that exist in our society create suspicion of immigrants and refugees, other races and religions, and those with nonconformist gender and sexual identities. We need to become a community that will build each other up and be welcoming, loving, and accepting of all people.

As discussed in chapter nine under Theology of Visibility, in Korea, the concept of *ou-ri,* translated as "our," is far more important than the individual. "Ourness" is a concept that has built up the Korean community with an emphasis on being connected to each other to protect and help others. *Ou-ri* in the Korean language is often used as a personal pronoun. So instead of saying "my family," in Korea, we say "*ou-ri* family." Instead of saying "my spouse," we say "*ou-ri* spouse," even though you are married to only one spouse. This different outlook and emphasis in life challenges us to become different individuals within the community, to prioritize the needs of the community. We need to adopt an *ou-ri*-ness in our theological journey so we can fight racism and overcome the other divisive beliefs we face as people of God. All people are invited to the banquet of God where we can dance, rejoice, and be merry in the presence of God. It is the *ou-ri*-ness of God's love that we should be embodying as Christians.

This recognition of the importance of community is what will lead us to seek changes in how we treat those within our communities who may not exactly fit the white male paradigm of Christianity. Communities are life-giving. Churches are a community of believers who work together to bring changes to help the marginalized, the oppressed, and the poor. As the faith community works together, they lift each other up and bring others into the community to intentionally build life-giving groups who can look out for each other, support one another and help one another.

Intentionally building communities will help us overcome the prejudices we may carry. If we build communities and groups that are supportive of each and every member, we can begin to eradicate the divisiveness of racism and sexism found in our churches.

DISCIPLESHIP

Discipleship is about growing spiritually as well as living out our faith lovingly in community. Discipleship is a journey of intentional decisions leading to a deeper relationship with Jesus and

God. It is about how we can become more faithful in all aspects of our lives. If we want to become more Christlike, we need to eliminate our racial and gender biases and welcome everyone as a child of God and part of the body of Christ. Discipleship means being intentional every day and being aware of our own biases that may get in the way of growing in our faith.

Discipleship is about cultivating Christlike character in ourselves. When we recognize patriarchal constructs and the alienation that creates in our churches and society, we can look to Jesus to see if he reinforced it or not. In the New Testament, we see over and over again how Jesus interacted with women and raised them up. Jesus conversed with and supported many women throughout the New Testament. In the story of the woman who anointed Jesus' feet, all the men in the house were upset at this woman's mere presence and became irate over her display of devotion to Jesus. But Jesus was not angry; instead, he welcomed it and said that we were to remember her actions because she demonstrated the kind of love he wants us to show one another. In other parts of the New Testament, we see that Jesus loved Mary and Martha and they became some of his closest friends. Jesus also talked to a Samaritan woman who was considered an outcast by her community. He told her about living water that would give her eternal life. Unlike the rest of society, Jesus did not set up barriers, oppress foreigners, nor subjugate women. Instead, Jesus did the opposite and praised the women around him. To grow in our discipleship, we need to do likewise. We need to become followers of Jesus and lift up the marginalized. By moving away from an image of a white male God, we can rid the church of the barriers, prejudice, and rejection of "outsiders" that is still so prevalent. It will help us to see how we are all important, valuable, and created in the image of God.

One way to evolve in our own discipleship is to keep a spiritual or discipleship journal. Journaling brings us into awareness and consciousness around our own habits, biases, and ways of being. It is a time and place to reflect on our faith journey and see what we have done and what we could do better. It will give you moments in the day to reflect and process events on a theological and spiritual level. You will deepen your spiritual walk and begin to understand your own actions and thoughts. You may begin to identify how you are moving beyond the white male God to a loving Spirit God who embraces all and who teaches us to do the same. Whether you write short entries every day or longer ones whenever you feel led, keeping a journal is an excellent tool that God can use to reveal insights and help you grow spiritually.

Perhaps you will use your journal as a place to write about times when you are confused or in wonderment, upset or joyful, grateful or sad. This is a place to help you process where God is and how you feel God's presence in your life. Keep it with you as you read and reflect on Scripture to understand what it means for us today. We need to reread and reconsider these texts to make sense of our different interpretations of scriptures. The way we interpret Scripture affects our discipleship. It will inform how we view God and how we live and become disciples of Christ.

The damage that the image of a white male God has done to people of color and to women has been enormous. We need to unlearn our ways of thinking and believing as we try to live a more faithful life, which means loving and embracing everyone. We need to live trustworthy lives as we struggle to understand God Spirit, who is merciful, welcoming, and embracing of everyone.

Discipleship is not just about knowing Christ; it is about doing something just, faithful, and life-giving. Discipleship takes a lot of maturity in our faith journey. It requires us to be disciplined in our life to work toward liberation and justice. A new discipleship in a faith that is nonwhite and nongendered is how we all will right the wrongs of generations of a distorted view of God.

JUSTICE WORK

The fundamental purpose of the shift in perspective I have called for in this book is to provoke us to work for a better society, church, and community—to build stronger, more equal, and more loving spaces that are just and liberative. We know that whiteness led to genocide, enslavement, indentured workers, Japanese internment, voting restrictions, segregation, and many more horrific injustices. Unpacking and removing whiteness from the church and from Christianity is a critical component for realizing justice, restoration, and some form of peace.

If we do not deconstruct the whiteness at the root of our churches, communities, and families, it will continue to destroy and separate us. We must create space for reimagining ourselves, creation, and God without the white male influence. As we do this, we must also guard ourselves against other frameworks becoming oppressive and destructive. Frameworks such as ethnocentrism can become problematic in every culture. We need to be vigilant and not allow other replacements that become self-centered, self-serving, and have no care or regard for others who may be different from us.

Justice work needs to be tangible and applicable. I am part of the Korean American Clergywomen's group within the Presbyterian Church (USA), and our group does our part to fight racism and patriarchy by naming them and being supportive of each other when we are confronted with these evils. A strong network of similar people fighting causes for justice will help work toward a more equal and just society.

At my own seminary, we required (but most recently elimi-nated the requirement from our curriculum) a crosscultural class. This was a travel course that required students to immerse them-selves in a culture and society other than their own. I was able to take white students to Korea to teach how other cultures practice and live out their Christianity and faith. In such a course, white students' biases and preconceived notions of nonwhite people were challenged and confronted. It became an overwhelmingly positive experience for them.

Intentional studying of different cultures and peoples helps eliminate prejudices of people of color. Seminaries and churches can celebrate Black History Month, Asian American Pacific Is-lander Heritage Month, Native American Heritage Month, and National Hispanic Heritage Month. These different forms of cel-ebrations in institutions and churches prioritize learning, cele-bration, and embracing of everyone.

Engaging in justice work requires our whole bodies—thinking of those who aren't like us as worthy, walking in marches and standing up for the marginalized, speaking up and reaching out to our representatives and lawmakers to create more just laws for the forsaken, voiceless, and oppressed. We need to be persistent, active, and strong when we engage in justice work, as it is a long process and a long journey to gain any form of justice.

We as a community of faith need to be engaged in many forms of justice work, recognizing the intersectionality of injustices. Women's issues are tied up with economic justice, which ties to racial oppression. Concerns over climate change reveal environ-mental racism and the barriers created by economic inequity. Gender identity restrictions impact women's rights, and so on. None of these injustices stand alone, and those affected by them should not have to stand alone either.

LAST THOUGHTS

The world is a diverse, complex, and nonhomogeneous place. We need to embrace the diversity present around us and rejoice in it, because God certainly does. We must recognize how our understanding of God affects our worldview, our actions, and our Christian faith. Our choice of words and the language we use impacts our thoughts and ideas. If we can move away from the false notion of a white male God, it will expand our understanding of the real God who is infinite and unrestricted. We need to explore and reimagine a God who is inclusive of all people no matter gender or racial identity, economic status, ability, or other distinguishing characteristics we may have. The more open our vocabulary and images as we come before God in prayer, readings, and songs, the better we will become. We cannot limit an infinite God with our limited choice of words and languages.

To move toward a more inclusive church and community, we will be better served by rewriting our liturgies, prayers, hymns, and worship guides with nonwhite and a nongendered words and concepts for God. This will create a major shift in our Christian identity and lived-out faith. It will teach and reinforce a God who is neither white nor male. This movement away from whiteness and patriarchy will open the door to a lived faith practice where how we treat one another is modeled after Jesus, who sought justice and liberation for all. The new possibilities and new hopes for a better church, community, and world are within our grasp if we are willing to reframe the God of our past and envision the kin-dom of God where we finally treat everyone as created in the image of God and as worthy, beautiful, and loved.

ACKNOWLEDGMENTS

People often ask me how I begin to write a book. Each author has different beginning points and reasons for writing a book. Most of my books are written to help me understand my own life experiences, contexts, and faith. This book is no exception. Writing this book helped me heal, make sense of my life, and move forward in rectifying some of the problems I saw in the church and society due to whiteness.

I am grateful to my community of friends and family that helped me reflect, understand, and write this book. They offered a sounding board for me to make sure my points are clear and my reflections are theologically sound. I am grateful for each friend who sustained me during this time of writing.

I am also grateful to Al Hsu, my editor with InterVarsity Press who shepherded me through the editing process of my book. This is my second book with Al—the first was *Healing Our Broken Humanity* cowritten with Graham Joseph Hill. It was a joy to work with Al on both of my IVP books. He is sharp, sensitive, and perceptive in developing further some of my ideas so that it is solid and comprehensible. I am so appreciative of his insights, suggestions, and ideas. I am also indebted to Cara Highsmith, who edited the first drafts of my book. With her assistance, this book became stronger and more accessible to all readers.

I cannot forget my family, who have encouraged me in writing this book. My children, Theodore, Elisabeth, and Joshua, are always so supportive in all my writing projects. My oldest son, Theo, really sparked the light in me to write this book quickly as he understood the importance of this project. I am happy that my husband, Perry, enjoys all my books and stood by me with this one too. It is my family that pushes me to continue to write and contribute to the theological world, which is dominated by white men. For that, I am always appreciative and grateful.

QUESTIONS FOR REFLECTION AND DISCUSSION

1. ENCOUNTERING WHITENESS

1. Name a time or an incident when you encountered whiteness. Did it make you uncomfortable or uneasy? Please share some of your feelings and experiences about encountering whiteness and how you dealt with it.

2. How did the concept of race emerge? Do you feel that this concept of race should be eliminated from our society? Why or why not?

3. Does race affect your faith or church community? Why or why not?

2. THE PROBLEM OF WHITENESS

1. What is white privilege? If you are white, have you been aware of your own white privilege? Justice work is to relinquish some of your own power. How can you try to eliminate white privilege in your workplace, neighborhood, and church?

2. How does white supremacy work to oppress people of color? How can we work toward dismantling white supremacy?

3. BECOMING A WHITE CHRISTIANITY

1. Did you know that Christianity had a long history of becoming white? How does this knowledge make you feel? Will it change how you worship God, think about God, or think of your own faith?

2. Is your church engaged in mission work? If so, where? From reading this chapter, do you think missionaries should be trained and prepared differently before they go out into the world?

4. A MISSIOLOGY OF WHITENESS

1. Asian Americans have a different oppressive history from other people of color. Has this chapter challenged your own biases, thinking, and views of Asian Americans?

2. Edward Said did some extensive research on Orientalism. When was your first encounter of this word, and does Said's work impact how you understand Asia? If so, how? Please share and discuss.

3. How are Asian Americans stereotyped? How can your own community and church break down stereotypes so that loving communities can be built up without any form of stereotyping?

5. CHRISTIANITY AND WHITENESS

1. How do racism and discrimination go hand in hand with whiteness and Christianity? Many of the North American churches have a deep racism problem. How can the church work toward eliminating racism from churches and communities?

2. Please share you own immigration histories whether from generations ago in your family or present day. If you don't

know your own immigration story, how do you feel about immigrating to another country, and how would that impact your faith and understanding of God?

3. White supremacy, white Christian nationalism, and a white Christianity are detrimental to communities of people of color. How can you and your faith community work toward dismantling this from within your own community, city, and beyond.

6. A WHITE JESUS

1. Did you ever feel that Jesus may not be white? If so, please share when you felt this and the impact of it on your faith development. Was it disturbing or liberating?

2. How can we correct this error of creating and worshiping a white Jesus?

3. Does reading this chapter change or challenge your or your faith community's understanding of Jesus?

7. A WHITE GOD

1. Many churches teach a white male God, which can be very problematic to people of color and to women. Should we move away from this image of God? If yes, how can we accomplish this?

2. The maleness and whiteness of God creates a context of bold racism and sexism as part of the everyday life of the church. How can we work toward dismantling racism and sexism in our churches and communities?

3. Do you know of other images or understandings of God that are not male and nonwhite? Please share and discuss these images.

8. THE PROBLEM OF A WHITE GENDERED GOD

1. In light of sexism, sexual violence, and atrocities committed against women in society and in the name of Christianity, it is necessary to move away from this gendered white understanding of God. How can the church do this so that worship, study groups, and fellowship can be a safe place for women?

2. How can we hold discussion groups and worship that centers on a nongendered God?

3. What are some of your reflections on the problem of a white gendered God?

9. LIBERATING WHITENESS

1. Christians need to engage in racial justice work to reverse the damages of creating a white Christianity and a white Jesus. How can we begin to do this?

2. How can the dominant white culture stand in solidarity with communities of color?

3. What are some of the liberative ways of understanding and worshiping God?

4. When was your first encounter with a Spirit God? Was it beautiful, scary, or liberating? Please share and discuss with your group.

5. How can the church practice and heed the Spirit's urgent call to engage in justice work?

10. EMBRACING A NONWHITE AND NONGENDERED GOD

1. Practice in your small groups or by yourself writing liturgy that is more inclusive and embracing of all people. Write

some prayers, confession of sins, and poems. Share them with your small group if you feel comfortable.

2. What other practices can you or your church engage in to work toward building a more just world?

3. Have you encountered a God who embraces all people regardless of gender, ethnicity, class, and ableism? How can we talk about this God in our families, churches, and communities so that it will be impactful to people who have been oppressed, marginalized, and dominated by society and by the church?

NOTES

1. ENCOUNTERING WHITENESS

[1]Teresa J. Guess, "The Social Construction of Whiteness: Racism by Intent, Racism by Consequence," *Critical Sociology* 32, no. 4 (2006): 653-54.

[2]Jemar Tisby, *How to Fight Racism: Young Readers Edition* (Grand Rapids, MI: Zonderkids, 2022), 32.

[3]"Whiteness," CARED (Calgary Anti-Racism Education), accessed May 24, 2022, www.aclrc.com/whiteness.

[4]Guess, "Social Construction of Whiteness," 654.

[5]Robert P. Baird, "The Invention of Whiteness: The Long History of a Dangerous Idea," *The Guardian*, April 20, 2021, www.theguardian.com/news/2021/apr/20/the-invention-of-whiteness-long-history-dangerous-idea.

[6]Baird, "Invention of Whiteness."

[7]Guess, "Social Construction of Whiteness," 664.

[8]Guess, "Social Construction of Whiteness," 664-65.

[9]"Slave Codes," *U.S. History Online Textbook*, accessed June 21, 2022, www.ushistory.org/us/6f.asp.

[10]Lisa Sharon Harper, *Fortune: How Race Broke My Family and the World—and How to Repair It All* (Grand Rapids, MI: Brazos Press, 2022), 91.

[11]Baird, "Invention of Whiteness."

[12]Guess, "Social Construction of Whiteness," 660.

[13]Baird, "Invention of Whiteness."

[14]Laurie L. Dove, "When Irish Immigrants Weren't Considered White," *How Stuff Works*, accessed June 21, 2022, https://history.howstuffworks.com/historical-events/when-irish-immigrants-werent-considered-white.htm.

[15]Nell Irvin Painter, "What Is Whiteness?" *New York Times*, June 20, 2015, www.nytimes.com/2015/06/21/opinion/sunday/what-is-whiteness.html.

[16]Painter, "What Is Whiteness?"

[17]"Whiteness," CARED.

[18]See Rosemary Radford Ruether, ed., *Gender, Ethnicity, and Religion: Views from the Other Side* (Minneapolis: Fortress Press, 2002), x-xi.

[19]Harper, *Fortune*, 176.

[20]Whiteness," CARED.

2. THE PROBLEM OF WHITENESS

[1]*Two Years and Thousands of Voices: What Community-Generated Data Tells Us About Anit-AAPI Hate*, Stop AAPI Hate National Report, July 2022, 2-3, https://stopaapihate.org/2022/07/20/year-2-report.

[2]A version of this story was first published in Grace Ji-Sun Kim, "White and Yellow: Overcoming Racism," *The Feminist Wire*, April 24, 2013, https://thefeministwire.com/2013/04/overcomingracism.

[3]See Joseph Cheah, *Race and Religion in American Buddhism* (New York: Oxford University Press, 2011), 132.

[4]See Gale A. Yee, "Where Are You Really From? An Asian American Feminist Biblical Scholar Reflects on Her Guild," in *New Feminist Christianity: Many Voices, Many Views*, ed. Mary E. Hunt and Diann L. Neu (Woodstock, VT: Skylight Paths, 2010), 79.

[5]Robert P. Baird, "The Invention of Whiteness: The Long History of a Dangerous Idea," *The Guardian*, April 20, 2021, www.theguardian.com/news/2021/apr/20/the-invention-of-whiteness-long-history-dangerous-idea.

[6]Lisa Sharon Harper, *Fortune: How Race Broke My Family and the World—and How to Repair It All* (Grand Rapids, MI: Brazos Press, 2022), 91, 176.

[7]Miguel De La Torre, *Decolonizing Christianity: Becoming Badass Believers* (Grand Rapids, MI: Eerdmans, 2021), 15.

[8]"Whiteness," National Museum of African American History and Culture, accessed May 24, 2022, https://nmaahc.si.edu/learn/talking-about-race/topics/whiteness.

[9]See www.timwise.org.

[10]"Whiteness," National Museum of African American History and Culture.

3. BECOMING A WHITE CHRISTIANITY

[1]"Jewish Palestine at the Time of Jesus," *Britannica*, accessed May 20, 2022, www.britannica.com/biography/Jesus/Jewish-Palestine-at-the-time-of-Jesus.

[2]Ewen MacAskill, "George Bush: 'God Told Me to End the Tyranny in Iraq,'" *The Guardian*, October 7, 2005, www.theguardian.com/world/2005/oct/07/iraq.usa.

[3]Miguel De La Torre, *Decolonizing Christianity: Becoming Badass Believers* (Grand Rapids, MI: Eerdmans, 2021), 20.

[4]Lisa Sharon Harper, *Fortune: How Race Broke My Family and the World—and How to Repair It All* (Grand Rapids, MI: Brazos Press, 2022), 90.

[5]Ania Loomba, *Colonialism/Postcolonialism*, 2nd ed. (London: Routledge, 2005), 8.

[6]Harper, *Fortune*, 58.

[7]Loomba, *Colonialism/Postcolonialism*, 8.

[8]Brian McLaren, *Do I Stay Christian? A Guide for the Doubters, the Disappointed, and the Disillusioned* (New York: St. Martin's Essentials, 2022), 33.

[9]Harper, *Fortune*, 58.

[10]Choe Sang-Hun, "A Brutal Sex Trade Built for American Soldiers," *New York Times*, May 2, 2023, www.nytimes.com/2023/05/02/world/asia/korea-us -comfort-women-sexual-slavery.html.

[11]Choe Sang-Hun, "A Brutal Sex Trade."

[12]Loomba, *Colonialism/Postcolonialism*, 92, 99.

[13]Harper, *Fortune*, 38.

[14]Mark Charles and Soong-Chan Rah, *Unsettling Truths: The Ongoing, Dehumanizing Legacy of the Doctrine of Discovery* (Downers Grove, IL: InterVarsity Press, 2019), 16.

[15]Charles and Rah, *Unsettling Truths*, 21.

[16]De La Torre, *Decolonizing Christianity*, 19.

[17]Kaitlin Curtice, *Native: Identity, Belonging, and Rediscovering God* (Grand Rapids, MI: Brazos Press, 2020), 23.

[18]Curtice, *Native*, 44.

[19]Charles and Rah, *Unsettling Truths*, 21.

[20]Curtice, *Native*, 27.

[21]Kimberlee Medicine Horn Jackson, "United States: Native American," in *Christianity in North America*, ed. Kenneth R. Ross, Grace Ji-Sun Kim, and Todd M. Johnson (Edinburgh, UK: Edinburgh University Press, 2023), 116.

[22]Curtice, *Native*, 50.

[23]Curtice, *Native*, 27, 50, 108.

4. A MISSIOLOGY OF WHITENESS

[1]"Crusades," *Britannica*, accessed July 23, 2022, www.britannica.com/event /Crusades.

[2]Brian McLaren, *Do I Stay Christian? A Guide for the Doubters, the Disappointed, and the Disillusioned* (New York: St. Martin's Essentials, 2022), 30.

[3]McLaren, *Do I Stay Christian?* 30, 33.

[4]"St. Francis Xavier (1506-52) Jesuit Missionary," December 3, 2012, www
.catholicireland.net/saintoftheday/st-francis-xavier-1506-52-jesuit
-missionary.

[5]Dae Young Ryu, "Understanding Early American Missionaries in Korea (1884–
1910): Capitalist Middle-Class Values and the Weber Thesis," *Archines de sci-
ences sociales des religions* 113 (January–March 2001): 93.

[6]"Pioneer Protestant Missionaries in Korea: Seoul/1887," William Elliot Griffis
Collection, Rutgers University, 2.

[7]Ryu, "Understanding Early American Missionaries in Korea," 100-101.

[8]Ryu, "Understanding Early American Missionaries in Korea," 102.

[9]Ryu, "Understanding Early American Missionaries in Korea," 111.

[10]Donald N. Clark, "Christianity in Modern Korea," *Education About Asia* 11, no. 2
(2006): 36.

[11]Kirsteen Kim and Hoon Ko, "Who Brought the Gospel to Korea? Koreans Did,"
Christianity Today, February 9, 2018, www.christianitytoday.com/history/2018
/february/korean-christianity.html.

[12]Ryu, "Understanding Early American Missionaries in Korea," 103-4.

[13]The cost of plastic surgery is unknown until you seek private consultation for
upcoming procedures. But procedures are multistep, which continues to add
to the cost of skin whitening and other skin treatments; see, for example,
www.vippskorea.com/non-surgical/drvipskin/whitening-skin.html.

[14]Paul D. Miller, "What Is Christian Nationalism?" *Christianity Today*, February 3, 2021, www.christianitytoday.com/ct/2021/february-web-only/what
-is-christian-nationalism.html.

[15]Miguel De La Torre, *Decolonizing Christianity: Becoming Badass Believers* (Grand
Rapids: Eerdmans, 2021), 58.

[16]Edward Said, *The Edward Said Reader* (New York: Vintage Books, 2000), 67-68.

[17]Said, *Edward Said Reader*, 93.

[18]Ania Loomba, *Colonialism/Postcolonialism*, 2nd ed. (London: Routledge,
2005), 43.

[19]Loomba, *Colonialism/Postcolonialism*, 48.

5. CHRISTIANITY AND WHITENESS

[1]Michelle Chen, "She Could Have Been Your Mother": Anti-Asian Racism a Year
After Atlanta Spa Shootings," *The Guardian*, March 16, 2022, www.theguardian
.com/us-news/2022/mar/16/anti-asian-racism-atlanta-spa-shootings
-anniversary.

[2]Teresa J. Guess, "The Social Construction of Whiteness: Racism by Intent, Racism by Consequence," *Critical Sociology* 32, no. 4 (2006): 661.

[3]"Whiteness," National Museum of African American History and Culture, accessed May 24, 2022, https://nmaahc.si.edu/learn/talking-about-race/topics/whiteness.

[4]Miguel De La Torre, *Decolonizing Christianity: Becoming Badass Believers* (Grand Rapids, MI: Eerdmans, 2021), 15, 105-6.

[5]Kaitlin Curtice, *Native: Identity, Belonging and Rediscovering God* (Grand Rapids, MI: Brazos Press, 2020), 38.

[6]De La Torre, *Decolonizing Christianity*, 58.

[7]De La Torre, *Decolonizing Christianity*, 14.

[8]Robert P. Jones, "White Christian America Needs a Moral Awakening," *The Atlantic*, July 28, 2020, www.theatlantic.com/ideas/archive/2020/07/white-christian-america-needs-moral-awakening/614641.

[9]Paul D. Miller, "What Is Christian Nationalism?" *Christianity Today*, February 3, 2021, www.christianitytoday.com/ct/2021/february-web-only/what-is-christian-nationalism.html.

[10]De La Torre, *Decolonizing Christianity*, 58.

[11]De La Torre, *Decolonizing Christianity*, 58.

[12]Miller, "What Is Christian Nationalism?"

[13]Grace Ji-Sun Kim, "Let the Holy Spirit Guide How We Talk About Race," *U.S. Catholic*, September 21, 2017, https://uscatholic.org/articles/201709/let-the-holy-spirit-guide-how-we-talk-about-race.

6. A WHITE JESUS

[1]V. M. Traverso, "What Did Jesus Really Look Like?" *Aleteia,* May 3, 2018, https://aleteia.org/2018/05/03/what-did-jesus-really-look-like.

[2]Traverso, "What Did Jesus Really Look Like?"

[3]Traverso, "What Did Jesus Really Look Like?"

[4]Anna Swartwood House, "The Long History of How Jesus Came to Resemble a White European," *The Conversation*, July 17, 2020, https://theconversation.com/the-long-history-of-how-jesus-came-to-resemble-a-white-european-142130.

[5]House, "The Long History."

[6]House, "The Long History."

[7]Richard Stockton, "Why Is the World Filled with Depictions of a White Jesus When the History Says Otherwise?" in *ATI*, November 21, 2021, https://allthatsinteresting.com/white-jesus.

[8]Christena Cleveland, *God Is a Black Woman* (New York: HarperOne, 2022), 39.

[9]Miguel De La Torre, *Decolonizing Christianity: Becoming Badass Believers* (Grand Rapids, MI: Eerdmans, 2021), 101.

[10]De La Torre, *Decolonizing Christianity*, 101.

[11]De La Torre, *Decolonizing Christianity*, 102.

[12]De La Torre, *Decolonizing Christianity*, 102.

7. A WHITE GOD

[1]Mary Daly, *Beyond God the Father: Toward a Philosophy of Women's Liberation* (Boston: Beacon Press, 1985), 19.

[2]Darth Vader is the most prominent evil character in the Star Wars movie franchise. Original trilogy villains such as Grand Moff Tarkin and Emperor Palpatine are white, but the one who stands out most prominently in the franchise is Darth Vader, who is dressed in black.

[3]Robert P. Jones, "White Christian America Needs a Moral Awakening," *The Atlantic*, July 28, 2020, www.theatlantic.com/ideas/archive/2020/07/white-christian-america-needs-moral-awakening/614641.

[4]Miguel De La Torre, *Decolonizing Christianity: Becoming Badass Believers* (Grand Rapids, MI: Eerdmans, 2021), 207.

[5]Kaitlin Curtice, *Native: Identity, Belonging and Rediscovering God* (Grand Rapids, MI: Brazos Press, 2020), 41.

[6]Nell Irvin Painter, "What Is Whiteness?" *New York Times*, June 20, 2015, www.nytimes.com/2015/06/21/opinion/sunday/what-is-whiteness.html.

[7]Grace Ji-Sun Kim, "Let the Holy Spirit Guide How We Talk About Race," *U.S. Catholic*, September 21, 2017, https://uscatholic.org/articles/201709/let-the-holy-spirit-guide-how-we-talk-about-race.

[8]Kim, "Let the Holy Spirit Guide."

[9]Christena Cleveland, *God Is a Black Woman* (New York: HarperOne, 2022), 39.

[10]De La Torre, *Decolonizing Christianity*, 7, 38.

[11]Brian McLaren, *Do I Stay Christian? A Guide for the Doubters, the Disappointed, and the Disillusioned* (New York: St. Martin's Essentials, 2022), 22.

8. THE PROBLEM OF A WHITE GENDERED GOD

[1]Simone de Beauvoir, *The Second Sex*, trans. and ed. H. M. Parshley (New York: Vintage Books, 1989), 78.

[2]bell hooks, *The Will to Change: Men, Masculinity and Love* (New York: Washington Square Press, 2004), 18.

[3]David Adams Leeming, *God: Myths of the Male Divine* (New York: Oxford University Press, 1997), 3.

[4]Leeming, *God: Myths of the Male Divine*, 4.

[5]Simone de Beauvoir, *The Second Sex*, 70-71, 77.

[6]Miguel De La Torre, *Decolonizing Christianity: Becoming Badass Believers* (Grand Rapids, MI: Eerdmans, 2021), 86-88.

[7]De La Torre, *Decolonizing Christianity*, 196.

[8]Christena Cleveland, *God Is a Black Woman* (New York: HarperOne, 2022), 16.

[9]McLaren, *Do I Stay Christian?* 51.

[10]David Biale, "The God with Breasts: El Shaddai in the Bible," *History of Religions* 21, no. 3 (1982): 250.

[11]Cheryl B. Anderson, *Women, Ideology and Violence: The Construction of Gender in the Book of the Covenant and Deuteronomic Law* (New York: Bloomsbury, 2004), 92.

[12]Melissa Raphael, *The Female Face of God in Auschwitz: A Jewish Feminist Theology of the Holocaust* (New York: Routledge, 2003), i.

[13]Raphael, *Female Face of God in Auschwitz*, 82.

[14]Jürgen Moltmann, *The Spirit of Life: A Universal Affirmation* (Minneapolis: Fortress Press, 2001), 48.

[15]Raphael, *Female Face of God in Auschwitz*, 82.

[16]Anderson, *Women, Ideology and Violence*, 92.

[17]Raphael, *Female Face of God in Auschwitz*, 82.

[18]Grace Ji-Sun Kim, *The Grace of Sophia* (Cleveland: Pilgrim Press, 2002).

[19]Gail R. O'Day, "The Gospel of John: Introduction, Commentary and Reflections," in *The New Interpreter's Bible: A Commentary in Twelve Volumes*, vol. 9, ed. Neil Alexander (Nashville: Abingdon Press, 1995), 506; and Sharon H. Ringe, *Wisdom's Friends: Community and Christology in the Fourth Gospel* (Louisville, KY: Westminster John Knox Press, 1999), 38.

[20]Daniel Jose Camacho, "John's Prologue and God's Rejected Children," *The Christian Century*, January 4, 2016, www.christiancentury.org/blogs/archive/2016-01/johns-prologue-and-gods-rejected-children.

[21]Camacho, "John's Prologue."

[22]Elizabeth A. Johnson, *She Who Is*, 10th anniv. ed. (New York: Doubleday, 1964), ccxv.

[23]Elisabeth Schüssler Fiorenza, *Jesus: Miriam's Child, Sophia's Prophet: Critical Issues in Feminist Christology* (New York: Continuum, 1994), 139.

[24]Sharon H. Ringe, *Wisdom's Friends: Community and Christology in the Fourth Gospel* (Louisville, KY: Westminster John Knox Press, 1999), 43; and Johnson, *She Who Is*, 97.

[25]For more information, visit Roman Catholic Women Priests website: www .romancatholicwomenpriests.org.

9. LIBERATING WHITENESS

[1]Christena Cleveland, *God Is a Black Woman* (New York: HarperOne, 2022), 17.

[2]James Cone, *The Cross and the Lynching Tree* (Maryknoll, NY: Orbis, 2013), xiii.

[3]Cone, *Cross and the Lynching Tree*, 4.

[4]Jonathan Sacks, *The Dignity of Difference: How to Avoid the Clash of Civilizations* (London: Continuum, 2002), 56, 208.

[5]Sacks, *Dignity of Difference*, 209.

[6]Grace Ji-Sun Kim, *Invisible: Theology and Experience of Asian American Women* (Minneapolis: Fortress Press, 2021).

[7]Joseph A. Adler, "Varieties of Spiritual Experience: *Shen* in Neo-Confucian Discourse," in *Confucian Spirituality*, vol. 2, ed. Tu Weiming and Mary Evelyn Tucker (New York: Crossroad, 2004), 121.

[8]Mary Evelyn Tucker, "Introduction," in *Confucian Spirituality*, vol. 1, ed. Tu Weiming and Mary Evelyn Tucker (New York: Crossroad, 2003), 25.

[9]Robert Cook, "Alternative and Complementary Theologies: The Case of Cosmic Energy with Special Reference to Chi," *Studies in World Christianity* 6 (2000): 180.

10. EMBRACING A NONWHITE AND NONGENDERED GOD

[1]Jann Aldredge-Clanton and Larry E. Schultz, *Inclusive Hymns for Liberating Christians* (Burnet, TX: Eakin Press, 2006). And also use Jann Aldredge-Clanton and Larry E. Schultz, *Inclusive Hymns for Liberation, Peace, and Justice* (Burnet, TX: Eakin Press, 2023).

[2]Wil Gafney, *A Women's Lectionary for the Whole Church: Year A* (New York: Church Publishing, 2021). See also Year B and Year W.

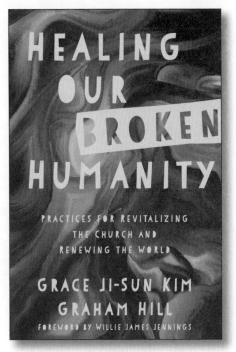

Healing Our Broken Humanity
978-0-8308-4541-5

Like this book?
Scan the code to discover more content like this!

Get on IVP's email list to receive special offers, exclusive book news, and thoughtful content from your favorite authors on topics you care about.

 | InterVarsity Press

IVPRESS.COM/BOOK-QR